DWELLING IN WONDER

Nature Journaling as a Spiritual Practice

Starr Regan DiCiurcio

Printed in the United States of America

Hardcover ISBN: 978-1-961624-55-9
Paperback ISBN: 978-1-961624-56-6
Ebook ISBN: 978-1-961624-57-3

DartFrog Plus is the hybrid publishing imprint of DartFrog Books, LLC.

301 S. McDowell St.
Suite 125-1625
Charlotte, NC 28204
www.DartFrogBooks.com

For my mother
Mildred (Milly) Dempsey Regan
1906-1986

When I was a child, she gifted me with a
Celtic experience of life's web.
She gently turned me to look over my right shoulder
at the new moon, and make a wish.
She taught me ladybugs bring good luck
and a bird in the house foretold a death.
And so much more...
Blessed!

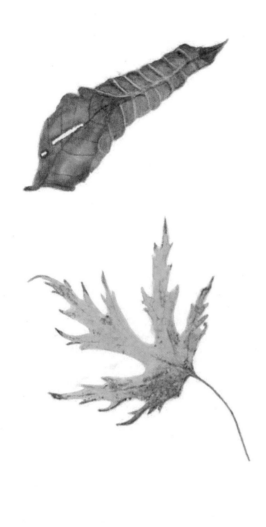

Contents

Foreword

Dwelling in Wonder: Nature Journaling as a Spiritual Practice is an invitation to explore nature through mindfulness. It brings together two practices, mindfulness and nature journaling, to enhance our connection to ourselves and the planet. Starr Regan DiCiurcio merges the practice of journaling and mindfulness, pathways to environmental awareness and wisdom.

As we explore nature, we may catch a glimpse of the wonder, mystery, and awe of this world. If we are also journaling, we slow down and our awareness of our surroundings and self deepens. This pause allows all our senses to open and what begins as a general recognition of beauty turns into a list of connections: the breeze on our skin, the warmth of the sun, the song of the robin, the yellow of the buttercup, the thrashing of the waves, the hush of snowfall, and so much more. Mindfulness supports these encounters with our wonder-filled world by keeping us present. It encourages us to let go of all distractions. When we choose mindfulness, we only hear the bird, the breeze, or the waves. We are not caught up in our concerns, regrets about yesterday, or worries about tomorrow. We choose our thoughts. These two practices mutually support each other as they increase our focus, awareness, and concentration. Mindfulness helps us journal, and journaling helps us be mindful.

Starr offers us a clear process for journaling mindfully. She also provides 365 daily prompts, an exploration of poetry, and a wellspring of inspiration. You will find a lot of encouragement in these pages. There are many concrete ideas for your nature journals no matter who you are, where you are, what your age, your interests, or abilities. Starr believes, as I do, that we all benefit from this process, and that all of us can do it. As you develop the tools of mindful journaling you will also grow in your love of this precious world of wonders. As we all learn to love this Earth with greater wisdom, may we wholeheartedly commit to her protection. We invite you to begin this journey.

John Muir Laws

Welcome Friends

If you love nature, you have picked up the right book. Welcome to the wondrous world of nature journaling as a spiritual practice. Here you will find the guidance you need to get started, plus many possibilities to explore as your journaling evolves. Perhaps you already keep a nature journal. Or perhaps you are curious about doing so. You may be a person of faith, or not. But if you have experienced awe standing in the hush of a first snowfall, viewing a colorful sunset, observing a wild creature, or gazing out to sea, you are ready to explore the spiritual side of nature journaling. The doors of the greatest of all cathedrals are open to you, the doors of Mother Earth.

You may already be coming up with limiting ideas that tempt you to declare nature journaling an impossible spiritual practice. But let's put some of those obstacles aside right away. You do not have to be a scientist or an artist. That said, I can promise that you will learn some science as you investigate what you observe. And you do not have to draw but if you do, it will be a profound way to learn about your subject. In nature journaling, we draw to become closer to the natural world around us. Anyone can draw. It is a skill that will develop if you give it a try.

You do not have to be an outdoorsperson or even go outdoors. If going outdoors is difficult, here you will find some ideas about how to reflect and journal on nature indoors. You do not have to devote hours every week to this practice. And if you feel you do not have time for one more thing, please consider the old Zen saying about sitting meditation. *If you feel you do not have 20 minutes to sit, you had better sit an hour.* The same goes for this spiritual practice. Invest in your own well-being.

I am an interfaith minister who often works as a spiritual director. Many people I sit with are disillusioned with their religious roots and carry deep spiritual wounds. Others are quite at home in their churches, temples, or synagogues, but wish to venture further in other wisdom traditions. More often than not, at some point in our conversations their love of this precious planet will come up. It usually takes the form of, "I feel closest to God (or the Divine, or Spirit, etc.) when I am (hiking, kayaking, watching birds, etc.). When we nature journal, we slow down and dive deep into those spiritual encounters. We dwell fully in the wonder of it all, returning as often as we wish. This nourishing practice can be life changing.

All nature journalers have their own stories to tell about coming to this practice. In my case, I can identify four roots supporting my experience. The first root is a deep love of nature that goes back as far as my memory does. As a young child I had the joy of growing up on the St. Lawrence River, spending every summer in the 1000 Islands. It is a spectacular waterscape and landscape that shaped in me an ever-growing love of water, mosses, kingfishers, Queen Anne's lace, herons, beavers, buttercups, turtles, all kinds of fish and so much more. That love has continued to expand over the years, especially in my ancestral homeland of Ireland.

For me, nature journaling is also sustained by a second root, contemplative practice. I am a longtime student of Buddhism and a minister who teaches meditation. As much as I treasure time with family and friends, I am most at home in quiet spaces. Writing is an expression of my love of solitude. So here is a third root. Words, my own and others', are on almost all of my journals' pages. There are labels, lists, and descriptions. If you enjoy poetry as I do, you will find material here on creating your own poems. It demonstrates just how easy that can be.

The fourth root of my nature journaling is a love of art. I had never given a thought to practicing art until I quite accidentally encountered mandalas and trained to be a facilitator. From there I went on to study botanical art which was challenging. I was taught by a wonderful teacher, Ida Mitrani, who provided skillful guidance and encouragement. Later I became a docent at our local museum, the Hyde Collection, which turned out to be a nourishing way to deepen my understanding of art.

By chance, I stumbled upon nature journaling on the internet through the outstanding work of John Muir Laws (www.johnmuir-laws.com). I was immediately attracted to it and incorporated it into my mindfulness practice. Because of these four roots, (love of nature, contemplation, writing, and art), I felt at home right away. Some people come to the practice of nature journaling with roots in the sciences, such as botany, forestry or meteorology. Others have valuable experiences in indigenous cultures that offer us all wisdom in this time of ecological crisis. Two of the strengths of this international community are the wide range of employed disciplines and the diversity of participants.

One root that we all have is our ancestry. Our family, whose blood flows in our veins, has its own particular history, its own traditions and wisdom. It may also carry trauma and other forms of suffering. All that comes to us through the generations is a valuable source of learning. We also have land ancestors, the people who lived on the land before us. We can trace that heritage back to indigenous peoples whose cultures and belief systems can help us heal our fractured relationship with nature today. Last of all, we can lean on our spiritual ancestors who brought wisdom and ethical guidance to us through the centuries. We can skillfully apply the teachings of these ancestors, (blood, land and spiritual), to the critical needs of our times. Some examples can be found in the section on wisdom traditions.

It is a source of joy to develop my practice, both on my own and in the worldwide community of nature journalers (www.wildwonder.org). The Covid pandemic opened up the opportunity to stay at home and dive more deeply into journaling. Now I want to share this practice so others can benefit from its richness. This is a time of crisis for our planet. Many of us are committed to helping in any way possible. Nature journaling is one way to do so. I nature journal to search my own soul for who I am, what I can give, and how I will do that. It is a deeply personal and private experience that I share in the larger community so I can continue to learn and develop my work. Such sharing is optional, but I have found it helpful and a source of encouragement and happiness. Nature journaling keeps me balanced so I do not despair when studying about deforestation, the loss of biodiversity, booming population issues, climate change, and more. It keeps me grounded.

You may feel that your journal could not possibly make a difference in this world. It can. Your journal, added to mine and thousands of others, can increase global understanding in our times. It can strengthen our communities as it educates people of all ages. It can bring clarity and deepen reverence. Ultimately, it contributes to raising us all to a higher level of consciousness that is necessary for the survival of humankind.

When I sit in nature with my journal and contemplate a majestic tree, fascinating flora and fauna, or the stars, the deepest part of me connects to all that is. It is an expansive opening. I experience the web of life in a direct way that elevates my soul. And I have hope. I wish you hope also. In this age of eco-anxiety, it is a needed act of courage. Come journal with me!

WHAT NATURE JOURNALING IS

- Deepening your connection to the natural world
- A private exploration of that relationship
- Self-expression in your chosen ways
- New learnings
- Words, numbers, and images
- Experiencing curiosity
- Inviting awe and wonder
- Connecting to the Divine
- Sharing in community—if you wish
- A practice across generations
- Fun!

WHAT NATURE JOURNALING IS NOT

- An invitation to your inner critic
- A playground for your judging mind
- All about expertise in science or art
- All about schedules or pressure
- Arduous
- Expensive
- Lonely

JANUARY
2023

Eastern White Oak
The 1st - 47° - Crandall Park
no snow

Lichens

- Lichens are neither plants nor animals.
- Lichens are a complex life form that is a symbiotic partnership of 2 separate organisms — a fungus & an alga.
- The fungus is dominant. It creates a more hospitable environment for the algae.
- There are 3,600 species in No. America.
- They grow slowly & live for thousands of years.
- They first evolved about 250 m. yrs. ago.
- They convert carbon dioxide in the atmosphere through photosynthesis into oxygen.
- They absorb pollutants.
- They are threatened by climate change.

W&N lemon yel deep
DV Fr. Ultramarine (red shade)
with white gouache

January 19th
Backyard Mosses

side

top

Crisped Pincushion
Ulota crispa

Tangled Thread Moss
Hygroamblystegium
varium

"Mosses & other small beings issue an invitation to dwell on a time right at the limits of ordinary perception. All it requires of us is attentiveness."
Robin Wall Kimmerer

Turkey tail fungi
Trametes versicolor
Fungi and lichens

This contemplation —
winter's stillness & beauty
restores the weary.

Jan. 23rd
Snow!

Materials For Nature Journaling as a Spiritual Practice

When you take up nature journaling as a spiritual practice, the requirements are simple. A notebook, pencil and eraser are all you need. As time goes on, you may wish to include a number of other supplies, but you may choose to keep it just that simple. Nothing else is needed except your nature subjects which are all around you.

I often depend on my phone's camera to record what I wish to include, or what I am considering for inclusion. This helps me remember details of color and form when I am completing my pages at home. If you are using a camera, be sure to do so in a contemplative manner. You are looking deeply, recording as much information as possible as you witness nature before you. Cameras are a great help when your time is limited by circumstances beyond your control, such as moving critters, fading sunlight or a waiting friend. Since we try to leave nature undisturbed by our presence, photographs are a vehicle for taking subjects home without causing harm.

You may want to see more than your human eyes allow. Binoculars are a great help. Be sure to get a pair that are lightweight and comfortable to use. A telescope can open up the gorgeous wonders of the Cosmos. To get up close, a magnifying glass or hand lens can also assist you. You may have access to one on a phone app. You may even want to employ a microscope. If you wish to look inside a subject, dissecting tools or a very sharp, small knife, will come in handy.

If you wish to study color, there are many options. Nature provides us with valuable information through color. Colored pencils are easy to use in the field and come in a wide variety. Artist pens that are lightfast and permanent are also easy to travel with. Markers and alcohol inks are other options. Watercolors provide a great range of colors and artistic expression. If that is a skill of yours or one you wish to pursue, you will need watercolor or mixed media paper, quality paints, paintbrushes, a water container, palette, rags or paper towels. A waterbrush is also a tool many journalers employ.

Other items you may wish to use are a ruler, magnifying lens, compass, stencils, or French curve. Phone apps offer a wealth of helpful information. The ones I rely on regularly are iNaturalist for plant and animal identification, and Cornell's Merlin Bird ID which is a rich resource on our feathered friends. More are included in the Daily Prompts section.

A folding chair or stool can make sitting outside for extended periods easier. If you are journaling at home, be sure to give yourself a comfortable seat in a good viewing spot. This could be simply in front of a window or on a deck or porch

You may wish to designate a carry case just for your journaling supplies. It should be light, weather resistant, and easy to carry, leaving your hands free. If all your supplies are in one place, it will be handy to grab them as you go out the door ready to explore. But remember, all you really need is your pencil, eraser and journal.

I wish you hope...In this age of eco-anxiety, it is a needed act of courage. Come journal with me.

The Spiritual Process of Nature Journaling

O ver the years, one thing I have learned as a spiritual director is that everyone is on a unique path. Even within the confines of a religious community, a ministry, or a complete rejection of belief, each one of us searches for life's meaning. How that search evolves varies as we strive to reach a place of integrity and inner freedom. Throughout this book you will see encouragement to trust your intuition and find your own way. That said, all of us benefit from the experience of others. Trying and rejecting ideas is helpful. All our forays teach us about ourselves and who we are in this place and moment in time. Everything fluctuates, including us. So, if an idea was worthless to you last year, it may be a gem now. Keep hearts and minds wide open.

What follows is my process of nature journaling. You can cherry pick, add to, or rearrange the particulars. Make it yours and give it a try.

Stopping

One of the most difficult things to do in these times is slow down and stop. This is meant literally. Stop moving. Stop thinking. Stop planning. Stop worrying. Stop. We are usually rushing. Our bodies often are, and even more so, our minds. Observe your daily patterns. Are you in touch with your inner world? Do you know yourself, your values? Can you let go of your concerns? Do you allow yourself to rest? Do you know how to follow your breath and relax? In order to employ nature journaling as a spiritual practice, you need to center yourself and let go of everything except this experience. It is a nourishing gift you are giving yourself and those around you. If on any particular day there is something that is especially preoccupying, sit with it for a few minutes and then let it go, knowing you can return to it later. You will return to it refreshed and bring new energy to the issue.

Setting Your Intention

This is simple. Just decide what your intention is for this time of journaling. It may be quite specific, such as learning about a species of tree new to you. It may be open ended, such as wanting to see what the park looks like today. Or it may be turned inward, such as quieting the churning mind that is finding stopping difficult. Recognize this as a time of learning and healing as you connect with nature and the Divine. Claim that for yourself.

Meditation

If your adventure includes a walk, try starting out in walking meditation. You do not have to change your normal pace. Just walk and observe your steps as they touch the Earth. This is an opportunity to recognize your connection with the planet as you gently touch your feet down with awareness. As you walk, turn your attention to your breath. Notice how many steps go with your in-breath and how many go with your out-breath. Then settle into that rhythm with awareness. Your mind will naturally calm. If you like, you can add a gatha, (a word or short phrase), for each step. You can write your own or try one of these.

- In, Out
- Oui, Merci
- Heal us, Bless us

Your walk may be short or long but try to continue in this manner. Your mind will relax, and you will be ready for the next step, contemplation.

Contemplation

Once you have settled in a place you wish to observe, you can turn your attention to the world around you. Your aim is to be pure presence. Invite your senses, one by one, to contemplate all that surrounds you.

Seeing

Our eyes are looking all the time, but how often do they really see? Bring your full awareness to what you are seeing now. Look at the big view, all that is around you. Then focus in on closeups of the many small details of life nearby. What is calling for your attention? It could be a mountain range, a pond, a rock or a pollywog. Decide. What will you be with now?

Hearing

Sounds surround us, even in times of dedicated silence. Close your eyes, if you wish, and listen. What do you hear? Can you identify any sounds? Are any produced by humans? What information is coming to you in this way? Just note.

Touching

The world of texture is rich and interesting. You may wish to touch the object of your focus. Is it strong or fragile? Is it cool or hot? Rough or smooth? Be sure it is safe to touch. You do not want a case of poison ivy as a memento. And of course, do not touch if doing so might harm the plant or little critter. Be aware that others may need this being. This biodiverse world is interdependent and precious.

Smelling

Note any smells. Are they pleasant, unpleasant? Constant or intermittent? What are the roles of any odors you notice? How would you describe them?

Tasting

Only indulge this sense if you know it is safe and not disruptive. Take note. Is it bitter? Sweet? Does it evoke memories? Is it appealing or not?

Noting

By now you probably have some idea of what you want to enter in your journal. You may be drawn to something that strikes you as exquisite. You may be drawn to something you have never seen before. Or it could be a being you want to learn more about, are afraid of, find mesmerizing or even are repulsed by. If you are fortunate to see a rare or endangered species, you will want to spend time with that precious opportunity. After carefully observing all the possibilities offered by your environment, it is time to choose what will go in your journal.

Investigating

You are now well settled in and ready to journal. Take out whatever materials you brought along. Rest in awareness of your subject. Perhaps you'll review your sense impressions again. Now look at the relationships you see. Whatever you are observing relates to others. Observe all the elements of relationships you can. For example, you might be watching a gray squirrel. Your eyes will follow it to a nearby tree. What kind of tree is it? What is the squirrel doing there? Is there a nest? Then you notice there is another squirrel, or is it the same one? What is in its mouth? Where is it taking it? What is that bare spot on its fur? Is that a parasite? And so on... You can also note changes in your subject. This could happen in one visit, or a series of visits to the same place, called a *sit spot*. For example, choose a tree and sit watching its leaves fall. What changes in the tree do you see? In the leaves? If you return every week over a season, you will be able to record remarkable changes in the tree and in its many relationships within its setting. Enjoy this time of focus, writing, and mark making.

Reflecting

Now your observations can slow, and you can come into a time of increased mental quiet. Let this be an opening to recognize nature's miraculous revelations. You have just seen a parade of miracles. Know that you are privileged to be the observer. You are part of this amazing web of life. Here is the wonder. Dwell in it. Note the characteristics of the objects of your investigation. You may have seen beauty, strength, courage, fragility, generosity, caring, or tenacity. If you witnessed killing, it will have been for food, not gratuitous or evil. Turn your attention to your own feelings. How did you feel before you started? How are you feeling now? Is there anything you would wish to do differently next time? Do you have questions to follow up on? Take notes in your journal.

Expressing Gratitude

Pause and remember how fortunate we are to be able to employ our senses and connect with the Earth. We are grateful for this time of exploring and learning. We are grateful for the solitude found in nature, and also for the opportunities to share our experiences with others. Finally, we recognize how blessed we are to live on this precious planet, including the small piece of it that offered today's sacred encounter.

Nature Journaling in Solitude and Community

Solitude and community are both pillars of spiritual life. In solitude, we come to know ourselves and the world we live in. If we are walking in the woods on a snowy day, we are struck by the beauty and silence around us. But as we listen, we become aware of many sounds. Ice cracks, the wind whispers, small animals scurry away and birds call. It is a symphony of creation. And since we are walking without human company, we can tune in to it all. We can observe our thoughts and get to know what is taking up space in our minds and hearts. Time such as this is a wellspring for creativity. We may stop and journal or take photos for journaling later in the warmth of our homes. Hopefully, we open to the wonder of the world around us and allow it to lift our hearts in praise and thanksgiving.

If we belong to a nature journaling group, we are fortunate. Many are online and offer a rich resource for new ideas of self-expression. Seeing how others compose their pages, use different media and approach their subjects, inspires us. Information becomes available about classes, excursions, teachers, apps, books and more. I am deeply grateful for the work of John Muir Laws. Jack is a gifted artist and scientist who is dedicated to bringing people all over the world to nature journaling. He is also a warm and kind person who is a joy to be with and to learn from. On his website, you can find many free resources including lessons on YouTube and materials for teachers. He also offers his books and nature journaling supplies there. Each year, Jack organizes a Wild Wonder Conference online with a diverse and informative lineup of experts. Don't miss it! If you are on Facebook, the Nature Journal Club, also organized by Jack and his team, is notable. You can see a wide variety of examples of journal pages by long time practitioners as well as beginners. It is a goldmine of ideas and everyone is so enthusiastic and encouraging. Take some time to get to know Jack's work and you will greatly benefit.

You are indeed lucky if you have found a nature journaling group that meets in person. A group can be organized as a club, workshop, or class. A club needs a facilitator to get things organized, but no one has responsibility for instruction. A workshop or class indicates a teacher. You can also opt for a hybrid. The group I belong to meets monthly on Zoom and field trips are offered whenever desired. It is a loose structure that serves us well. There is a list of groups on the website of The Wild Wonder Foundation (www.wildwonder.org). If you do not find a group near you, just gather a few like-minded friends and begin your own.

There is enormous support in belonging to a community. We encourage one another and keep each other on track. It is helpful if everyone can avoid judgment of their own or others' work. It is one thing to look at how a page could be improved, and another to discredit the work done. We are usually hardest on ourselves. And the issue I see arising too often is the comparing mind of journalers deciding that their own work does not measure up. We all have things we wish we could do better, but the real danger is giving up. Celebrate what you and your fellow journalers can do. Remember the greatest gifts of nature journaling are found in the process, not the product. Stay with the process and value it. Practice will make all our charts, graphs, drawings, writing and lettering better. Keep it joyful and playful to go the distance. Remember your journal is for you and you alone. Sharing is a rich opportunity, but it is also optional. Share when you are ready to share. Watch your self-talk. Be as positive as you would be when talking to a loved one. In a group, it is essential that everyone is careful when commenting on each other's work – which we only do when invited. Here are some guidelines.

Guidelines for Sharing Nature Journals

1. Always be kind. Be an encourager of yourself and others!
2. Be mindful of the time so everyone has a chance to share.
3. There is no pressure to share.
4. If you have a suggestion, ask if the creator wants to hear it.
5. Begin and end with positive comments.
6. Be curious. Ask questions.
7. Avoid comparisons.
8. If making a suggestion, phrase it in terms of your own work. "If this was my page, I think I would..."

9. Do not interrupt creators when they are presenting their work. Save your comments and questions until the end.
10. If something is unclear, ask for clarification. It probably is unclear to others.
11. Remember to handle all creative works with reverence.
12. If anyone asks for a sharing to be confidential, that request will be honored by all present.

It is engaging to open your nature journaling gatherings with a poem or reading that relates to your topic, if one is designated. You might consider taking turns offering the opening words. At the end of your meeting, you may conclude with a prayer that leaves everyone hopeful and inspired to journal. Here is one for you.

Concluding Prayer

We bow in gratitude for this sacred time we have shared.

Let us be enlightened by one another and the wise ones.

Let our teachers be the sky above us, the wind around us and the earth beneath us.

Let us learn from the mighty sea and the meandering stream.

Let us learn from the swaying grasses, the prickly plants, the glorious flowers, and the mighty trees.

Let us learn from the four-legged ones, the winged ones, the finned ones, and the creepy crawlies.

Let us rejoice in the beauty of the bounty we inhabit.

Let us become its protectors, its stewards, its servants, its lovers.

We bow before all that is, knowing we are eternally moving in divinity and divinity is within each one of us.

Amen

Turkey tail fungi
Trametes versicolor
Fungi and lichens

This contemplation –
winter's stillness & beauty
restores the weary.

Your journal is yours and yours alone. It is to be shared only when, where, and with whom you want. It is an extension of you and is precious in itself.

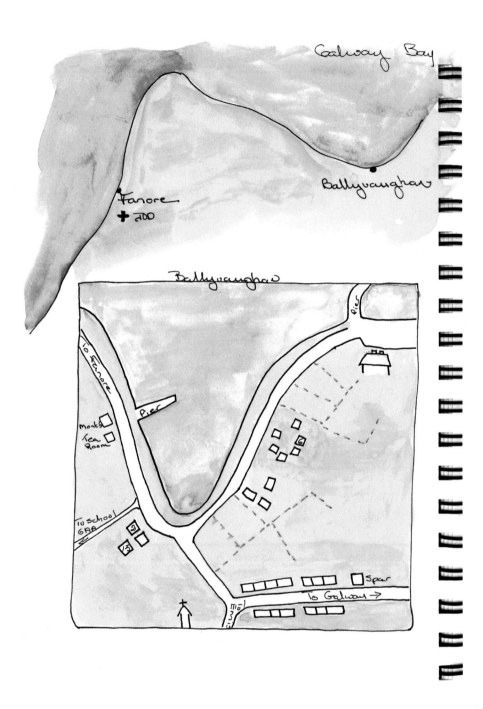

Galway Bay

Ballyvaughan

Fanore
✝ 200

Ballyvaughan

Pier

To Fanore

Monks
Tea Room

Pier

To School
GAA

Spar

To Galway →

To Ennis

Keeping Safe Outdoors

When you venture into the field for nature journaling there are a few things to keep in mind.

Here is a checklist:

- Plan your outing. If the territory is new to you, have a map and be aware of landmarks to look for as you go.
- Know if you will have cell phone service.
- Charge your phone.
- Take enough food and water if you will be gone for an extended period.
- Take a buddy with you, but do not depend on that friend for essential information. Always assume you might have to navigate on your own.
- Let someone know your plans before you leave home, including an expected return time.
- Take bug spray. Know if there are ticks in your area and, if so, examine yourself for them on return.
- Take sunscreen and a first aid kit as needed.
- If you are near ocean waters, know the time of the tides. Plan accordingly.
- Know the hour you will lose daylight.
- Watch for slippery surfaces.
- Be aware of any poisonous plants or fungi in the area.
- Be aware of any animals in whose territory you are going.

When you are well prepared, relax and have a great adventure!

Spore Prints

1. Cut stem off mushroom.
2. Place cap on black paper. (Use white paper for dark spore mushrooms.)
3. The spores drop out, leaving a print.
4. Spray with a fixative.

Basic Mushroom Parts

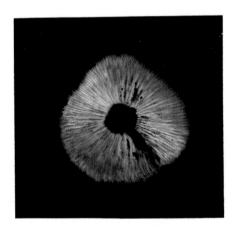

One Mushroom, Three Ways

Nature Journaling in Interesting Places

There are times when we may wish to look for new venues for our nature journaling practice. This may be due to limiting circumstances, or simply the weather. In the Northeast of the US where I live, there are long winters. And although they offer many subjects for observation, it can be a pleasant change to experience nature indoors. We might also want to switch up our routines to stimulate our thinking and broaden our awareness of the beauty and wonder of this world.

If you are venturing out to nonpublic places, be sure to call ahead and get permission to journal there. Some might not welcome visitors, although I have never encountered that response. Others might be open to journalers, but only during certain hours or on certain days. Be sure to ask if there are restrictions on the materials you can work with while visiting. Some museums for example, will only allow pencil drawing.

Investigate the area where you live for new, interesting opportunities. Once you open your search, many options will start to appear. Here are a few ideas:

- garden centers,
- natural history museums,
- universities,
- estate or castle gardens,
- humane aquariums and zoos
- bike & hiking trails
- environmental centers,
- parklands,
- onboard boats or ships,
- farms,
- community gardens,
- urban streets & vacant lots,
- planetariums,

- the meditation gardens of churches, temples, or other spiritual centers,
- monasteries.

Many of these venues offer programs that might interest journalers. Check out their calendars. Be sure that any aquarium or zoo you visit is ecologically responsible and humane. Natural history museums have amazing finds such as fossils, preserved animals and birds, and skeletons of extinct animals. You can plan to enjoy some extra time of contemplation in the meditation gardens of monasteries which are well designed for this. Monastery grounds usually include some vegetable and fruit gardens, often located in delightful settings.

Nature Journaling at Home

Usually when we talk about nature journaling, we think about time in the great outdoors. We picture journalers walking in parks or taking hikes into incredible landscapes. There they find a place to sit, contemplate and record in their journals. But is this a limiting vision? I think so. As valuable as these traditional approaches are, it is possible to journal outside these boundaries.

Many of us enjoy hours in nature, observing new and old friends we find there. We take notes, sketch, carefully photograph and return home with ideas for pages dancing in our heads. In the comfort of our homes, pages are created from scratch or finalized. This is my preferred way to journal, but I am flexible with it all, creating an experience that is first and foremost meditative and relaxing. Often, time in nature is a time of contemplation, meditation, or prayer. Where better to connect to Spirit than in the natural world?

But for many people excursions into nature are not possible. Whole communities do not see this nourishing and life-changing practice as attainable. There are ways they can be included. Here are some groups we can reach out to:

- the differently abled,
- those going through illness,
- those homebound,
- those caring for others,
- those with mobility issues,
- the imprisoned,
- urban dwellers,
- those with dementia,
- the very young and the aged.

Perhaps the most important help we can offer to people facing such restrictions is to show them the real possibilities of nature journaling indoors, at home or in a facility. There are ways to easily open opportunities for many. Here are some suggestions:

Sitting Outside at Home

Some fortunate potential journalers have access to a yard or even a garden, but they do not think of it as a world of wonder to explore. In fact, even a small yard can offer ample opportunity to observe and record the lives of plants, trees, insects, fungi, butterflies, birds and so much more. A container garden on a deck and some bird feeders can also do the trick. These are rich avenues of reflection, research and journaling.

The Window

Another option is a window where the journaler can sit and observe. Be sure the seat is comfortable for extended times of contemplation and observation. If the window opens to a garden, park or trees, it is a bonanza. But even if it seems not to hold any promise, there is much to pursue. A bird feeder can be attached to the window. Watching feathered beings live between the worlds is fascinating and joyful. The sky can be the subject of an entire journal. Sunrises, sunsets, clouds, lightning, and the stars, moon, and planets of the night sky – all are inspiring subjects. The changeable weather creates great opportunities for recording scientific data and reflecting on our role here on Earth.

The Kitchen Goldmine

Much of the food we ingest comes from the natural world. You may even be a plant-based eater. Here again we can dedicate a whole nature journal to a home-based opportunity. Open your refrigerator and see if there are items you wish to include. If not, add a few interesting fruits and vegetables to your shopping list. Or simply take the humble tomato off your windowsill and draw it. Slice it in half and draw the cross section. Is there a stem, a leaf? Draw them. Take a cross section of a purple cabbage and look at the beauty there. Do some research on land practices, organic farming, local vs. non-local produce, industrial farming, the treatment of animals, and more. You can also explore the history and practices around food in spiritual traditions. What have you learned? One topic will naturally lead to another. What would you like to put in your journal? It can be fun to take a favorite recipe and break down its component parts in drawings and text. Perhaps there is some family history connected to it. Put it all in your journal.

Houseplants

If some of us are unable to get out into nature, houseplants are a way to bring nature in. There are so many intriguing options, and they go through many processes that can be recorded: birthing, budding, branching out, infestation, decaying and dying. There are some interesting options with bonsai and terrariums. If you are giving a plant gift with journaling supplies, be sure that the care requirements of the plant meet the interest and abilities of the recipient. It's more fun that way.

The Nature Table

A nature table holds objects of nature that you can safely store at home. If you have space, you can set up a permanent nature table. If space is limited, you can place your collection of treasures in boxes and pull out items when you wish. Some suggestions for collecting are birds' nests, shells, dried fungi, pinecones, bark, dried flowers, rocks, hornet nests, leaves, nuts, seeds, grasses, fossils, deceased bugs and butterflies. The nature table is a great resource for journaling. It gives you time with the subjects. Examining a dead butterfly is much easier than examining a flitting one! Collecting items for your table is a rewarding activity. Be careful not to cause any disturbance when you remove an item from its natural environment.

Pets and People

Don't forget that your beloved pets are part of nature too. You can record their habits and idiosyncrasies. Fish, cats, dogs, hamsters, birds, guinea pigs, rabbits and other sentient beings are valuable for your scientific study, as well as companionship.

For some people, it can be a stretch to recognize yourselves as part of nature. But we are indeed part of the web of life, dependent on all other components of our environment, as they depend on us. Your journal can be a place to record all change: illness, birth, diseases, rates of growth, and more. Learn through research, as well as direct observation of the dynamic, glorious universe you move in and are forever a part of.

So if you, or someone you know, becomes confined to indoor spaces or a yard, look for ways to broaden the horizons. Sit at the window and watch the industrious dedication of a spider as she spins her web. Record the changing colors of a maple tree. Nature journaling is available to you. Don't give up. Even if you are bedridden, a single plant, a bouquet of flowers or a tray of food, can become a new world to explore. This practice is yours to create for your own edification and elevation of spirit. All are welcome to nature journaling!

Bodhi
Beautiful
Blind
Beloved
9-11-2005 ● 9-25-2021

Red squirrels are native to Ireland. Their habit of hoarding seeds and nuts are important to the ecosystem. They have been in decline since the arrival of the grey squirrel a century ago. But Fr. Christopher explained that the recovery of the pine marten is bringing the grey squirrel pop. into balance & reducing the threat to the red squirrels.

Rules! Rules! Rules!

Both journaling and spirituality are fields ripe for the creation of rules. You will find many "shoulds" if you take classes, read books, join groups or surf the web. There is a goldmine of inspiration as well as information in these resources, but please avoid the rules.

For this practice of spiritual nature journaling, free yourself from restrictions. Well intentioned guidance can be too narrow and prescriptive. Your own intuition and experience will be your best teachers, along with the natural world itself. Keep open to new adventures in self-expression. If things do not go as you anticipated or wished, you can learn something from that. There are no failures, only lessons.

That said, rules can be incredibly helpful. These rules are the ones you set yourself. They can help give you a nourishing, centered, and soulful experience. I set some guidelines that serve me well. Yours will probably look different, but here are two of mine: Rule 1. My journal is limited to what I actually observe. This is a way to establish some parameters on the topics I include. The erupting volcano on the news may be fascinating but it won't go in my journal. However, the chipmunk on my porch will get a place. Rule 2. I keep all my pages. My journal is a bound book of watercolor paper. It allows me to use the watercolors I greatly enjoy, but it also does not allow me to easily remove pages. It might be possible to carefully cut one out, but I have made a rule for myself not to do that. Perfectionism is a trap I can fall into, and this rule keeps me from ending up with an empty journal. My journaling often doesn't go as I envisioned, but I find ways to adjust and accept the lessons. And next time I face a similar challenge, I have a page to help me avoid that particular pitfall. There are journalers who use a ring binder. That would never work for me. I could write and draw for years and end up with a sad paucity of pages. So, find the rules that work for you, and then always remember that your rules are made to be broken!

And here's another important reminder. Your journal is yours and yours alone. It is to be shared only when, where, and with whom you want. It is an extension of you and is precious in itself.

APRIL

A Lantern Poem
Line 1 - One syllable noun
Line 2 - Describe ↑ 2 syllables
Line 3 -   "   3   "
Line 4 -   "   4   "
Line 5 - Synonym for noun Line 1
            1 syllable

Buds
Bursting
All around.
Greening the earth.
Joy!

Forsythia - Bud to Bloom

Pussy Willows

Poetry for Your Journal

Words are one of the pillars of nature journaling, along with numbers and images. They are like the three legs of a stool, each supportive of one another and necessary to the whole. Descriptions, labels, lists of researched or observed facts, are all pretty straightforward. We aim for clarity and accuracy with these words. When we reach into the world of poetry, we aim differently. Engaging with poetry, as a writer or a reader, often employs our imagination, our emotions and our spirituality. Poetry employs the observed material world to reach beyond, and encapsulates profound truths that inspire our thoughts and actions.

There are great poets who address the natural world in their work. If you read them, you will find lines of poetry to enrich your own journal pages. And unless you are publishing your journal and have copyright concerns, go ahead and use them. Of course, it is good manners to note the attributions. Here are just a few of the many poets who have inspired me:

- Matsuo Basho
- Wendell Berry
- Lucille Clifton
- Emily Dickinson
- Robert Frost
- Joy Harjo
- Major Jackson
- Ada Limon
- Naomi Shihab Nye
- Mary Oliver
- John O'Donohue
- William Shakespeare
- Henry David Thoreau

The poems that will best express your heart are your own. You may hesitate to write poetry if it is new to you, but please don't. It can be a great source of satisfaction and even fun. The structure of specific formats, such as haiku, will give you helpful starting points. But do not let the rules inhibit your joy in writing or your ability to express yourself. You can leave all the rules behind and go straight to free verse. Remember this is your journal and yours alone. Create it as a reflection of your heart and mind. The following pages contain some poetic possibilities to encourage and inspire you. They are suggestions to hold lightly.

Haiku

You are probably familiar with haiku. This simple Japanese poetic form is popular in school curriculums, and you might have learned it as a young student. It has a long history but was refined and popularized by Basho in the 1600's.

Here is the suggested format:

Line 1 – 5 syllables

Line 2 – 7 syllables

Line 3 – 5 syllables

If you are uncertain about syllables, check a dictionary where words are broken into them. More importantly, haiku aim to create images from nature. Employ your senses. Here are two examples from my journals. Each is repeated with syllables noted.

Wisteria charms,
dropping her lavender self
from the strength of vines.

wis-ter-i-a charms (5)
drop-ping her la-ven-der self (7)
from the strength of vines. (5)

Childhood memories

spring up with Indian Pipes –
God's gift this fine day.

child-hood me-mor-ies (5)
spring up with In-di-an Pipes – (7)
God's gift this fine day. (5)

Lantern

A lantern poem is a winsome addition to your nature journal. It utilizes both words and images. After you have the words, you can organize them to fit inside a lantern of your design. Once again this form of poetry is a gift to the world from Japan. In that culture, lanterns represent good luck and happiness. To all of us, they symbolize the coming of light. For this reason, you may find it especially meaningful to include lantern poems when you are journaling on dark, winter days or welcoming the longer days of springtime.

Here is the format:

Line 1 – noun 1 syllable

Line 2 – 2 syllables to describe the noun

Line 3–3 syllables to describe the noun

Line 4 – 4 syllables to describe the noun

Line 5 – 1 syllable synonym for the noun

Here's my example:

Buds
bursting
all around.
Greening the earth.
Joy!

You can create any lantern design you wish, but here are some possibilities. [add templates]

Acrostic Poems

Acrostic poems take a word and expand on its theme. It may be especially meaningful when you are moved by the beauty of something you encounter, or when you are grieving a loss in the world of nature. It may be a reminder of an aspiration that you wish to keep before you. Like previous formats, no rhymes are required. Simply write your chosen word vertically on the page and then expand from each letter into a word or phrase.

Here's one from my journals built on the word reverence:

R esting
E nchanted—
V enerating
E very
R eality
E ntered
N ow—
C reation
E xalted

Barnacle

A barnacle is a contemporary Irish poetry form. It is named in honor of James Joyce's muse, Nora Barnacle. The progression of lines suits nature journaling well.

Here is the format:

Line 1 – literal expression

Line 2 – emotional expression

Line 3 – spiritual expression

Here's my example that features nature in Ireland:

Imbolc brings the glowing light of spring –
An invitation to freshness, creativity, and joy.
Come dance down Brigid's sacred path of wonder.

Free Verse

Free verse has no rules: no rhyme, no meter, no format. It is your own expression of your experience without any dictates. Here are two of mine.

Lessons

Creation is the teacher of us all.
Her lessons lead inexorably toward love,
far, far away from lurking isolation and trepidation.
I, student of all that is, open my senses to Her.

Let me see the lesson of
    the sunrises' faithful promise.
Let me hear the lesson of
    the thunder's timely warning.
Let me feel the lesson of
    the lost fawn's trembling heart.
Let me smell the lesson of
    the skunk's spray of fear.
Let me taste the lesson of
    the Earth's bountiful fruits.

And when the lessons are learned:
Let me honor faith.
Let me heed warnings.
Let me protect the lost.
Let me relieve all fear.
And let me bow in gratitude before Earth's bountiful fruits.

Soul Friend

There are days...
hard, hard days.
My steps unsure,
my memories painful,
my heart worn,
my mind unclear.

Let me lean on you awhile.
Let my face feel your bark.
Let my eyes watch your leaves dance.
Let my feet steady on your roots.
Let my soul trust our sacred bond.

Eastern White Oak

The 1st - 47° - Crandall Park

no snow

White Tailed Bumblebee

Over 20,000 bee
species in world.
98 in Ireland.
WTB - 3 identical species that
can only be separated by DNA.
Bumblebees, unlike honeybees, do not store
food. Always close to starvation.
They provide invaluable pollination service
to plants. Very friendly & not aggressive.

St. Gobnait
Patron Saint of bees
and beekeepers
Feb. 11th Saint day

Sunrise
1-5-22

Zoom In, Zoom Out

An Introduction to Meditations on Nature

Mindfulness is an essential component of nature journaling. It brings us into the present in a deliberate, sustained manner. This quality of awareness is the basis for meaningful observations. Mindfulness calms and centers us. It frees our minds from the tugs of the past and the pulls of the future. It is a spiritual practice and an important tool of science.

Meditation is not essential to nature journaling, but it supports our experience of mindfulness. Some of the known benefits are physical, such as lowered blood pressure and heart rates, reduced fear, anxiety, stress and pain, and improved immune systems, concentration and memory. The brain experiences important gains, such as increased neuroplasticity, thicker cortical walls and synchronization of the left and right hemispheres. Other benefits include increased creativity, resilience, and awareness. Many people meditate for these good reasons. Others meditate as a spiritual practice, a way of grounding and deepening their connection to Higher Consciousness. Probably, most of us meditate for a combination of reasons.

If meditation is already part of your life, or if you would like to give it a try, the following examples are included for you. Of course, you do not need any words at all to mediate. Meditating in silence is powerful. As Mother Teresa said, *We need to find God, and he cannot be found in noise and restlessness. God is the friend of silence. See how nature – trees, flowers, grass – grow in silence; see the stars, the moon, the sun, how they move in silence. We need silence to be able to touch souls.* Especially our own.

Not everyone is comfortable in silence. Many of us find meditation difficult in complete quiet. So guided meditations offer us words to help us settle in. Often after a guided meditation, it is possible to relax into silence. The words can act as a kind of bridge. There are apps available you might like to try. Insight Time and Plum Village are both free. Two others that are excellent, but charge a fee, are Headspace and Calm.

In the following meditations, my words focus on the natural world to complement our journaling experience. Some of them begin with two verses taken from the traditional Buddhist meditation on the breath as practiced in the community of Thich Nhat Hanh. (You can see this clearly in the meditations on the seasons.) The last meditation is on hope which is the critical state of mind we need to maintain as we keep informed about the environmental crisis.

You may meditate before you begin journaling, as a break, or as a concluding wrap up. You may meditate walking, sitting, lying down or standing. You may meditate for five minutes or an hour. Enjoy it. That is the only requirement.

Walking Meditation

A Meditation on the Elements

Meditation on Winter*

Meditation on Spring*

Meditation on Summer*

Meditation on Fall*

Meditation on the Cosmos

Tree Meditation

Flower Meditation*

Meditation on Hope

*Previously published in *Divine Sparks: Interfaith Wisdom for a Postmodern World*

Walking Meditation

Aware of this sacred space, let me pause. Releasing the day – all the concerns, the preoccupations, the habits of my mind. Entering fully into this moment, this place.

May my footsteps be gentle.
May they carry me toward beauty and truth.

As I walk, let me turn myself over to the walking, trusting it fully to carry me forward. There is nothing else to do. Just walk.

May my footsteps be gentle.
May they carry me toward beauty and truth.

Here there is no destination, no agenda, no obstacles, no dead ends. There is only the earth supporting me, holding me in faith.

May my footsteps be gentle.
May they carry me toward beauty and truth.

As life's busyness falls away, there is an opening. A pause that brings clarity and promise. I become aware of the glory of the planet, and realize I am its child.

May my footsteps be gentle.
May they carry me toward beauty and truth.

My heart swells in gratitude for the wonder of nature's mystery. Thankful for the legs that carry me, I walk for those who cannot.

May my footsteps be gentle.
May they carry me toward beauty and truth.

My gratitude extends to all the land ancestors who walked this ground before me. May I learn their lessons of living in harmony with all beings. May my own blood ancestors walk with me also, and may I live in a manner that protects this planet for those coming after me.

> May my footsteps be gentle.
> May they carry me toward beauty and truth.

Walking in peace.

Walking in joy.

Walking in wonder.

> May my footsteps be gentle.
> May they carry me toward beauty and truth.

A Meditation on the Elements

Breathing in, I calm my mind.
Breathing out, I open my heart.
In, out.

Breathing in, I am aware of Interbeing.
Breathing out, I am part of Interbeing.
Aware of Interbeing, part of Interbeing.

Breathing in, I bow to Earth, Wind, Fire and Water.
Breathing out, I smile to Earth, Wind, Fire and Water.
Elements around me, elements within me.

Aware of the element of earth,
I bow in gratitude.
Earth of desert sands, rocky ocean shores, and snow-capped
    mountains.
Earth, rich loam, nurturer of plants, fungi, and trees.
Earth, home of worms, chipmunks, foxes, and bears.
Earth of my bones,
I bow in gratitude.

Aware of the element of wind,
I bow in gratitude.
Wind, carrier of autumn leaves, germinating seeds, and sweet
    pollen.
Wind, lifter of birds, butterflies, kites and sails.
Wind, air of my breath,
I bow in gratitude.

Aware of the element of fire,
I bow in gratitude.
Fire, giver of light – candles, bonfires, stars and sun.
Fire, giver of warmth at welcoming hearths on cold winters'
    nights.
Fire, preparer of nourishing foods for bountiful tables.
Fire, warmth of my body,

I bow in gratitude.

Aware of the element of water,
I bow in gratitude.
Water of gently flowing streams, tranquil lakes, mighty rivers and
    majestic seas.
Water, giver of life to all plants, animals and sentient beings.
Water, crystal clear delight.
Water of my tears and my blood,
I bow in gratitude.

Aware of Spirit,
I bow to the Great Mystery –
The intricate orchestrations of all the elements of creation.
I honor these gifts that manifest my life ---
From ladybug to elephant,
From starfish to whale,
from bud to bloom,
from chirp to thunderclap,
from breeze to typhoon,
from spark to blaze,
from droplet to deluge,
from the mosses under my feet to all my fellow beings,
To the stars, the galaxies, the universe.

I dwell in beauty.
I dwell in awe.
I pray my praise.
I commit to love.

Meditations on the Seasons

Introduction

The following meditations are based on the four seasons. Of course, our experience of the seasons varies greatly with where we are located geographically, but the meditations are meant to acknowledge the passing of time, our connection to the rhythms of nature, and our impermanence. Most of all, they offer praise for the beauty around us and its divine source.

Meditation on Winter

Breathing in, I know I am breathing in.
Breathing out, I know I am breathing out.
In, out.

Breathing in, my breath goes deep.
Breathing out, my breath grows slow.
Deep, slow.

Breathing in, I enter stillness.
Breathing out, I calm.
Stillness, calm.

Aware of the season of winter,
I contemplate interbeing.
Winter, interbeing.

Aware of darkening days,
I invite deep rest.
Darkening days, deep rest.

Aware of birds migrating south,
I see empty perches.
Migrating birds, empty perches.

Aware of hibernating creatures,
I hear silence.
Hibernating creatures, silence.

Aware of fallen leaves,
I see space between tree branches.
Fallen leaves, space between tree branches.

Aware of flowers turned to compost,
I see sleeping gardens.
Flowers turned to compost, sleeping gardens.

Aware of ice on rivers,
I know fish swim in deep waters.
Ice on rivers, fish swimming.

Aware of birds leaving,
I see birds arriving.
Birds leaving, birds arriving.

Aware of bare tree branches,
I hear sap running.
Bare tree branches, sap running.

Aware of slumbering flowers,
I know seeds are preparing to burst forth.
Slumbering flowers, seeds preparing.

Aware of winter present,
I feel spring emerging in winter present.
Winter present, spring emerging.

Winter present, spring present.
Quiet rest of dark days,
entering light.

Meditation on Spring

Breathing in, I know I am breathing in.
Breathing out, I know I am breathing out.
In, out.

Breathing in, my breath goes deep.
Breathing out, my breath grows slow.
Deep, slow.

Breathing in, I enter stillness,
Breathing out, I calm.
Stillness, calm.

Aware of the season of spring,
I contemplate interbeing.
Spring, interbeing.

Aware of the coming of light,
I rejoice.
Coming of light, rejoicing.

As the days lengthen,
the sun warms.
Lengthening days, warming sun.

Little bells calling us to worship.
Snowdrops appear, call to worship.

Crocus then arrive in a blaze of color,
a balm to winter's white.
Crocus color, winter's white.

Flocks of winged ones fill the sky.
Birdsong lifts my heart.
Flocks of winged ones, birdsong.

Mud season has arrived.

Now in nature, now in me.
Mud season in nature, mud season in me.

Out of this primordial darkness,
comes endless beauty.
Out of darkness, beauty.

From inner darkness,
shines my true inheritance, my divine spark.
Inner darkness, divine spark.

Springtime is renewal.
Springtime is promise.
Renewal, promise.

All of creation infused with life,
manifesting divine intention.
Infused with life, manifesting divine intention.

Winter receding, spring arriving.
Winter receding, spring arriving.

Meditation on Summer

Breathing in, I know I am breathing in.
Breathing out, I know I am breathing out.
In, out.

Breathing in, my breath goes deep.
Breathing out, my breath grows slow.
Deep, slow.

Breathing in, I enter stillness.
Breathing out, I calm.
Stillness, calm.

Aware of the season of summer,
I contemplate interbeing.
Summer, interbeing.

Days have come into fullness,
full of light,
full of warmth.
Light, warmth.

Aware of the sun's blessings,
I bask in long days,
In generous, radiant days.
Long days, radiant days.

Aware of sunny days,
my energy surges forth,
my heart sings.
Surging energy, heart singing.

This is the season of water,
refreshing, cool water,
inspiring water.
Cool water, inspiring water.

Running streams, raging rivers, languid lakes –
All present their summer gifts to me.
I receive them joyfully.
Summer gifts, receiving joyfully.

Mighty ocean, source of all life,
mesmerizes and enchants us.
I am drawn to its shore again and again.
Mighty ocean, enchanting ocean.

Aware of the sounds of summer
I hear music everywhere –
children playing, birds call, cicadas' song.
Sounds of summer, music everywhere.

Sudden storms arrive with drama --
thunderclaps, lightning strikes
and the descent of rain's refreshment.
Sudden storms, refreshing rains.

Aware of the energy of summer days,
I hear heat's invitation to rest.
Hammocks, beach blankets and porches call.
Summer's energy, call to rest.

Aware of the gift of long days,
I can embrace play
and its nourishment of laughter.
Play, laughter.

Aware of the Earth's greening
I see her glory in full bloom.
Greens of emerald, lime, forest, olive and mint.
Earth's greening, full bloom.

Summer is the time of my greening too.
I come into the fullness of these days
with openness, gratitude and joy.
Greening summer, gratitude and joy.

Autumn will come bearing her own gifts.
The seasons cycle in a dance of reassuring rhythm.
Seasons cycle, reassuring.
Summer ending, autumn arriving.

Meditation on Fall

Breathing in, I know I am breathing in.
Breathing out, I know I am breathing out.
In, out.

Breathing in, my breath goes deep.
Breathing out, my breath grows slow.
Deep, slow.

Breathing in, I enter stillness.
Breathing out, I calm.
Stillness, calm.

Breathing in, I feel the freshness of fall.
Breathing out, I smile.
Fall's freshness, smile.

Leaves shine with color's glory,
Red, gold green, yellow.
Shining leaves, color's glory.

Leaves fall with ease and grace,
offering themselves to the earth.
Leaves falling, offering themselves.

Streams ripple and bubble –
flowing around stones in their path.
Streams ripple, flow around.

Nuts fall, squirrels gather --
preparations for winter begin.
Gathering nuts, preparing for winter.

Autumn's winds bring cool air,
Energizing, nourishing, cleansing.
Autumn's winds, cool air.

High in the sky birds migrate
seeking safety and warmer climes.
Birds migrate, seeking safety.

Days shorten cloaking us in darkness,
harbingers of winter to come.
Shortening days, winter coming.

Autumn fleeting, winter arriving --
seasons turning in beauty.
Faithful autumn, faithful winter.
Faithful autumn, faithful winter.

Meditation on the Cosmos

Breathing in, I feel the air enter my body.
Breathing out, I release.
Air entering, releasing.
Air entering, releasing.

Turing inward, I breath into my heart space.
Touching my center, releasing.
Touching my center, resting.
Releasing, resting.
Releasing, resting.

Behind closed eyes, I enter darkness.
Sheltering darkness, warm darkness.
In the quiet, I float
Ascending on the air surrounding me,
Bringing me between worlds.

The vastness of space invites me.
Space within, space without.
The ancient song of the universe sings to me.
Light pours from sunbeams and moonbeams,
Soft light, sparkling light, radiant light.
Soft light, sparkling light, radiant light.

Here is the peace of solitude.
Here is the peace of solitude
In the midst of teeming creation.
Here is the comfort of pattern
And the relief of patterns broken.
Constellations and shooting stars.

The surprise of color breaks through –
Violet, red, yellow, blue, orange, green –
Flashes of joy erupting spontaneously,
Sparking the dance of imagination.

Floating on the Milky Way
Stars sparkle into eternity.
Timelessness.
Cradled as in a holy mother's arms,
Peace within, peace without –
The universe within, the universe without.

Touching transcendence.
Breathing in freedom, breathing out joy.
Breathing in freedom, breathing out joy.
Breathing in freedom, breathing out joy.

Tree Meditation

Close your eyes and imagine you are walking into a beautiful park. It may be a park known to you, or a creation of your mind's eye. As you walk, notice all the living beings around you – grass, flowers, small animals, birds, butterflies, dragonflies, leaves, ponds and streams. What else do you see? Just slowly walk and enjoy the images that come to you.

Now select a tree that you feel drawn to. It can be any tree – one that was a childhood friend, one that you have studied or briefly visited, or one that appeared in your dreams. Walk slowly toward your tree.

As you approach the tree, notice her height and width. She may be a delicate tree or a giant. She is yours. Reach out and touch her gently. What does she feel like? Is she smooth or rough? What are the many colors of her bark? Place your ear near the tree. Can you hear any sap? Do other sounds come into your awareness?

Look down toward the earth. Imagine the large network of roots, soil and fungi that are below the surface. Feel their powerful network as they support the entire tree, the surrounding trees, the bushes, and other plants. They are supporting you too. Lift your gaze and look at the area around your tree. Can you see all the surrounding greenery, the *veriditas*, that is connected to your tree's roots? Is there a fallen limb nearby? It is offering a home to so many – worms, bees, spiders, moths, centipedes, beetles – a multitude of small creatures. This dead wood is also supportive of otters, hedgehogs, pine martens, bats, red squirrels, and many birds. Alive or dead, trees are essential to the forest, to life. Can you see how all is connected?

Now raise your eyes to the branches of your tree. What do they look like? Can you feel them reaching toward the sky? Can you feel their connection to the sun? Can you feel your connection to the sun? As you gaze at the tree's limbs, are there leaves, nests, birds, bees, and other living beings? Are squirrels chasing and playing above you? So many make their home here.

Look for evidence of the tree's bounty. Fruit. Nuts. Sap. Bark. Wood. So much food and medicine come from your tree. Bring your attention to the invisible gift of oxygen. Our lives depend on it, and here is the source. We offer the gift of our exhalations to the tree, sending carbon dioxide to nourish it. We inter-are in the most fundamental, critical way. A deep bow of gratitude.

Now imagine a storm approaching. It's becoming dark; the wind picks up and soon you feel the danger of violent weather. Lean right into your tree. Feel its strength and lifeforce. Breathe into it. Let the tree, from her deepest roots to her tallest branch, shelter you, as she shelters so many. Know that the tree is standing with the wisdom of the ages. She is stable and resilient. She perseveres through all. Let your tree gift you with those same powers.

Stability

Wisdom

Perseverance

Beauty

Nobility

Feel the strength of the tree in your body's core. Absorb it. Claim it as your birthright.

Now relax as you feel the wind subside and the storm pass over. Breathe into this tree that is your close relation. Offer gratitude. Gratitude for the many gifts you have received from countless trees throughout the years. Offer a promise to the trees. A promise of protection and support.

Returning to our breath, we breathe in.

Filled with oxygen, we breathe out.

Breathing in, breathing out.

Experiencing our connection with all that is, we breathe in.

Honoring our connection with all that is, we breathe out.

Breathing in, breathing out.

Deepening our gratitude for all life forms, we breathe in.

Living in awareness of all life forms, we breathe out.

Breathing in, breathing out.

Flower Meditation

Introduction

Choose a flower that draws your attention. Do this intuitively, without a lot of thought. One stem is enough. Now set it up in a way that you can easily see it in meditation without moving your eyes or changing the position of your body. You are ready to begin.

Turn your attention to your breath. Let yourself relax into the breath for a few minutes.

Now look at your flower. What is its color? What is its shape? Follow the lines of the flower's form with your eyes.

Can you smell the flower? If so, what is your experience of the scent? Do any judgments arise? Let them go.

Let gratitude for this flower enter your being. Feel it swell your heart as you contemplate the beauty, strength and healing powers of this small plant.

The flower does not come to you alone. It brings its roots and the rich soil that birthed it. It brings the sun and the rain that feeds it.

Together we share the same home—Mother Earth.

Together we share the warmth and light of the sun.

Together we share the nourishment of the rain.

Now soften your gaze and relax into your breath as you breathe with the flower.

As you connect your breath to the flower, be aware that this part of creation is supporting you and your breath.

Soften your gaze further or close your eyes.

Invite the flower's healing energy into your heart.

Feel the grace of its form.

Feel the glory of its color.

Feel the strength of its beauty.

Sit in silence with your flower.

Now slowly come back to the presence of your flower. When you are ready, deepen your breath, lift your eyes and come fully into the room.

Bow in gratitude to this small, precious being.

Meditation on Hope

Breathing in, I know I am breathing in.

Breathing out, I know I am breathing out.

In, out.

In, out.

In, out.

Touching the darkness of our world, I breathe in.

Contemplating the darkness of our world, I breathe out.

In, out.

In, out.

In, out.

Touching the darkness within me, I breathe in.

Contemplating the darkness within me. I breathe out.

In, out.

In, out.

In, out.

Sitting with darkness, without and within, I breathe in.

Releasing darkness without and within, I breathe out.

In, out.

In, out.

In, out.

Inviting hope, I breathe in.

Choosing hope, I breathe out.

In, out.

In, out.

In, out.

Nourishing hope, I breathe in.

Strengthening hope, I breathe out.

In, out.

In, out.

In, out.

Hope brought by a cool breeze,

a soaring bird, a reaching tree,

a shining star, a chant,

a symphony, or a tin whistle.

Hope on a candle's flame,

A butterfly's wings, or a sunflower's face.

Hope on a waterfall's song

or the hush of midnight.

Hope on my heartbeat,

Hope on my breath,

Hope on every new dawn.

Inviting hope, I breathe in.

Choosing hope, I breathe out.

In, out.

In, out.

In, out.

May my footsteps be gentle.
May they carry me
toward beauty and truth.

Autumn Haiku
Your dream dress is gone.
Yet quiet beauty lingers.
Not quite finished yet.

November 2022

Glens Falls

You may be a person of faith, or not. But if you have experienced awe standing in the hush of a first snowfall, viewing a colorful sunset, observing a wild creature, or gazing out to sea, you are ready to explore the spiritual side of nature journaling.

Nature in the Wisdom Traditions

Religious tradition is one of humanity's great sources of inspiration, solace and ethical guidance. If you were raised in such a heritage, you may wish to explore its reflections on nature and humans' relationship to nature, of which we are all a part. Or perhaps you are interested in looking at other spiritual writings and what they offer. I encourage you to do so. What we find is that across traditions the teachings have much in common, and can be a source of connection and growth toward understanding for both us and the planet. As you investigate, there may be words that concern you, such as the idea that nature was created to serve humankind. When we run up against teachings that make us bristle, it is an opportunity for us to clarify our thinking. The words, and your reflections on them, make rich additions to your nature journal.

I have chosen a variety of quotes to share from a number of wisdom traditions. They are meant to be a springboard for you. You can extend this small collection through your own experience and research. Quotes will inspire your journaling and, perhaps, acts of service.

You may wish to incorporate a reading in your prayers. For this, *lectio divina* is a rich and nourishing practice that comes down to us over the centuries. It's format may vary, but here are the steps I enjoy:

1. Read the text.
2. Reflect on it and see if a particular word or phrase draws your attention.
3. Read the text a second time.
4. Pray in any way that feels right to you.
5. Sit in silence.

Enjoy your exploration of the wisdom traditions and your practice of *lectio divina*. Let the beauty of the natural world and the insight of the ancestors nourish you.

Indigenous Wisdom

The Honorable Harvest, a covenant of reciprocity between humans and the land as found in *Braiding Sweetgrass* by Robin Wall Kimmerer of the Citizen Potawatomi Nation

> "Ask permission of the ones whose lives you seek. Abide by the answer.
> Never take the first. Never take the last.
> Harvest in a way that minimizes harm.
> Take only what you need and leave some for others.
> Use everything that you take.
> Take only that which is given to you.
> Share it, as the Earth has shared with you.
> Be grateful.
> Reciprocate the gift.
> Sustain the ones who sustain you, and the Earth will last forever."

Chief Seattle (?-1866) Suquamish Tribe

> "Teach your children
> what we have taught our children –
> that the earth is our mother.
> Whatever befalls the earth
> befalls the sons and daughters of the earth.
> If men spit upon the ground,
> they spit upon themselves.
>
> This we know.
> The earth does not belong to us,
> we belong to the earth.
> This we know.
> All things are connected
> like the blood which unites one family.
> All things are connected.
> Whatever befalls the earth
> befalls the sons and daughters of the earth.
> We did not weave the web of life;
> we are merely a strand in it.

Whatever we do to the web,
we do to ourselves..."

Max Dulumunmun Harrison, Aboriginal Elder of Australia (1936-2021)

"So, I take this word reconciliation and I use it to reconcile people back to Mother Earth, so they can walk this land together and heal one another because she's the one that gives birth to every-thing we see around us, everything we need to survive."

The Hindu Tradition

Sukla Yajur, Veda XXXVI

O God, scatterer of ignorance and darkness,
grant me your strength.
May all beings regard me with the eye of a friend,
and I all beings!
With the eye of a friend may each single being
regard all others!

Hindu Prayer

May the axe be far away from you,
May the fire be far away from you,
May there be rain without storm,
Lord of Trees, may you be blessed,
Lord of Trees, may I be blessed.

Atharva Veda XIX

Peace be to the earth and to airy space!
Peace be to heaven, peace to the waters,
Peace to the plant and peace to the trees.
May all the powers grant to me peace!
By this invocation of peace may peace be diffused!
By this invocation of peace may peace bring peace!
With this peace the dreadful I now appease,
With this peace the cruel I now appease,
With this peace all evil I now appease,
So that peace may prevail, happiness prevail!
May everything for us be peaceful!

Srimad Bhagavatam 11.2.41

A devotee should not see anything as being separate from the
Supreme Personality of Godhead, Krishna. Ether, fire, air, water,
earth, the sun, and other luminaries, all living beings, the direc-
tions, trees, and other plants, the rivers and oceans – whatever
a devotee experiences he should consider to be an expansion of

Krishna. Thus, seeing everything that exists within creation is the body of the Supreme Lord, the devotee should offer his sincere respects to the entire expansion of the Lord's body.

Mahatma Gandhi (1869-1948)

What we are doing to the forests of the world is but a mirror reflection of what we are doing to ourselves and to one another. The good man is the friend of all living things.

The Buddhist Tradition

Sutta Nipata, 143-52

In safety and in Bliss
May all creatures be of a blissful heart
Whatever breathing beings there may be
Frail or firm... long or big... short or small
Seen or unseen, dwelling far or near
Existing or yet seeking to exist
May all creatures be of a blissful heart

From *Love Letter to the Earth* by Thich Nhat Hanh

... I don't think God is an old man with a white beard sitting in the sky. God is not outside of creation. I think God is on Earth, inside every living being. What we call "the divine," is none other than the energy of awakening, of peace, of understanding, and of love, which is to be found not only in every human being, but in every species on Earth. In Buddhism, we say every sentient being has the ability to be awakened, and to understand deeply. We call this Buddha nature. The deer, the dog, the cat, the squirrel, and the bird all have Buddha nature. But what about the inanimate species: the pine tree in our front yard, the grass, or the flowers? As part of our living Mother Earth, these species also have Buddha nature. This is a very powerful awareness which can bring us so much joy. Every blade of grass, every tree, every plant, every creature large or small are children of the planet Earth and have Buddha nature. The Earth herself has Buddha nature, therefore all her children must have Buddha nature, too. As we are all endowed with Buddha nature, everyone has the capacity to live happily and with a sense of responsibility toward our mother, the Earth.

The First Mindfulness Training based on the First Precept of the Buddha, Plum Village Community of Thich Nhat Hanh

Reverence For Life
Aware of the suffering caused by the destruction of life, I am committed to cultivating the insight of interbeing and compassion and learning ways to protect the lives of people, animals, plants,

and minerals. I am determined not to kill, not to let others kill, and not to support any act of killing in the world, in my thinking, or in my way of life. Seeing that harmful actions arise from anger, fear, greed, and intolerance, which in turn come from dualistic and discriminative thinking, I will cultivate openness, non-discrimination, and non-attachment to views in order to transform violence, fanaticism, and dogmatism in myself and in the world.

The Fourteenth Dalai Lama

"It seems that with development, the whole world has become much smaller, but the human consciousness is still lagging behind. If we want a better future, we must examine our mind-set now. We need to recognize our nature and then, if we have the determination, there is a real possibility of transforming the human heart. Compassion, loving-kindness, and altruism are the keys not only to human development but also to planetary survival. Real change in the world will only come from a change of heart. What I propose is a compassionate revolution, a call for radical reorientation away from our habitual preoccupation with self. It is a call to turn toward the wider community of beings with whom we are connected, and for conduct which recognizes others' interests alongside our own... Everything is interdependent, everything is inseparable. Our individual well-being is intimately connected both with that of all others and with the environment within which we live."

The Jewish Tradition

Isaiah 55:12-13

You will go out in joy
and be led forth in peace;
the mountains and hills before you
will burst into song,
and all the trees of the field
will clap their hands.
Instead of the thorn
will grow the cypress,
and instead of briars
will come up the myrtle.
This will be for the glory of the Lord,
for an everlasting sign
which will not be destroyed.

The Book of Job 12:7-9

Ask the animals, and they will teach you.
Ask the birds of the air, and they will tell you.
Ask the plants of the earth, and they will inform you.
Ask the fish of the sea, and they will declare to you.
Who among you does not know that the hand of the Lord has
    done all this?

Isaiah 11: 6-9

The wolf shall live with the lamb;
the leopard shall lie down with the kid;
the calf and the lion will feed together,
and a little child shall lead them.
The cow and the bear shall graze;
their young shall lie down together;
and the lion shall eat straw like the ox.
The nursing child shall play over the hole
of the asp,
and the weaned child shall put its
hand on the adder's den.

They will not hurt or destroy
on all my holy mountain,
for the earth will be full of the
knowledge of the Lord
as the waters cover the sea.

Hasidic Saying

When you walk across the fields with your mind pure and holy,
then from all the stones, and all growing things, and all animals,
the sparks of their soul come out and cling to you, and then they
are purified and become a holy fire in you.

The Talmud

Every blade of grass has a constellation in the heavens that strikes
it and says, Grow! Grow!

The Christian Tradition

Matthew 6: 28-29

Consider the lilies of the field, how they grow: they neither toil nor spin; and yet I say to you, that even Solomon in all his glory was not arrayed like one of these.

Hildegard of Bingen (1098-1179)

I am the one whose praise echoes on high.
I adorn the earth.
I am the breeze that nurtures all things green.
I encourage blossoms to flourish with ripening fruits.
I am led by the spirit to feed the purest streams.
I am the rain coming from the dew that causes the grasses to
    laugh with the joy of life.
I am the yearning for good.

Francis of Assisi (?-1226)

...Praised be you, my Lord, with all your creatures,
especially Sir Brother Sun,
who is the day through whom You give us light.
And he is beautiful and radiant with great splendor.
Of You Most High, he bears the likeness.

Praised be You, my Lord, through Sister Moon and the stars.
In the heavens you have made them bright, precious, and fair.

Praised be You, my Lord through Brothers Wind and Air,
and fair and stormy, all weather's moods,
by which You cherish all that You have made.

Praised be You, my Lord, through Sister Water,
so useful, humble, precious, and pure.
Praised be You, my Lord, through Brother Fire,
through whom You light the night
and he is beautiful and playful and robust and strong.

Praised be You, my Lord, through our Sister Mother Earth
who sustains and governs us,
producing varied fruits with colored flowers and herbs...

Pope Francis' Encyclical *Laudato Si*

We are not faced with two separate crises, one environmental
and the other social, but rather one complex crisis which is
both social and environmental.

There can be no renewal of our relationship with nature without
a renewal of humanity itself. Nobody is suggesting a return to
the Stone Age, but we do need to slow down and look at reality
in a different way.

What kind of world do we want to leave to those who come after us, to
children who are now growing up? We have only one heart, and the
same wretchedness which leads us to mistreat an animal will not be
long in showing itself in our relationships with other people. Every
act of cruelty towards any creature is contrary to human dignity.

The Islamic Tradition

Quran 6:38

All the beasts that roam the earth and all the birds that wing their flight are communities like your own.

Quran 16:65

And Allah has sent down rain from the sky and given life thereby to the earth after its lifelessness. Indeed, in that is a sign for a people who listen.

Sayings of Mohammad

If the Hour of Resurrection comes, and one of you is holding a sapling, finish planting it.
There is a reward for serving any living being.
No doubt, every one of you is a shepherd and is responsible for his flock.

Hafiz (1325-?) Sufi Poet

And still, after all this time,
The sun never says to the earth,
"You owe me."
Look what happens with
a love like that.
It lights the whole sky.

The Taoist Tradition

Lao Tzu (dates uncertain but perhaps 5th or 6th century BCE)

Nature does not hurry,
yet everything is accomplished.

Excerpts from the *Tao Te Ching* (trans. Stephen Mitchell)

29
Do you want to improve the world?
I don't think it can be done.

The world is sacred.
It can't be improved.
If you tamper with it, you'll ruin it.
If you treat it like an object, you'll lose it.

78
Nothing in the world
is as soft and yielding as water.
Yet for dissolving the hard and inflexible,
Nothing can surpass it.

The soft overcomes the hard;
the gentle overcomes the rigid.
Everyone knows this is true,
but few can put it into practice.

51
Every being in the universe
Is an expression of the Tao.
It springs into existence,
Unconscious, perfect, free,
Takes on a physical body,
Lets circumstances complete it.

Li Po (701-762) Chinese Poet and Taoist

You ask
why I perch
on a jade green mountain?
I laugh
but say nothing
my heart
free
like a peach blossom
in the flowing stream
going by
in the depths
in another world
not among men

The Jain Tradition

Acaranga Sutra 1.4.111-2

Ahimsa – All breathing, existing, living, sentient creatures should not be slain, nor treated with violence, nor abused, nor tormented, nor driven away. This is the pure, unchangeable, eternal law, which the enlightened ones who know have proclaimed.

Mahavira (6th cen.)

One who neglects or disregards the existence of earth, air, fire, water, and vegetation disregards his own existence which is entwined with them.

Jain Scriptural Aphorism

Parasparopagraho jivinam
All life is bound together by mutual support and interdependence.

The Confucian Tradition

Confucius

Let the states of equilibrium and harmony exist in perfection, and a happy order will prevail throughout heaven and earth, and all things will be nourished and flourish.

All things are nourished together without their injuring one another. The courses of the seasons, and of the sun and moon, are pursued without any collision among them. The smaller energies are like river currents; the greater energies are seen in mighty transformations. It is this which makes heaven and earth so great.

Excerpts from *The Western Inscription*, Zhang Zav (1020-77) Neo-Confucian

Heaven is my father and earth is my mother and even a small creature as I, finds an intimate place in their midst.

Therefore, that which extends throughout all the universe I regard as my body and that which directs the universe, I consider my nature.

May we strive together to make this glorious planet a peaceful place of sanctuary for all beings.

Daily Prompts for Your Nature Journals

D aily prompts are suggestions to peruse and enjoy. They range widely from scientific observations, inspiring people, holiday recognition, quotes, expressions of gratitude and praise, and much more. Each month provides a list with suggestions for you to explore. Just one could be your subject for the entire month. You might challenge yourself to do them all, or you might do none. They are designed to be a resource you can turn to again and again.

The months are arranged by seasons in the Northeast of the United States where I live. If you live in the southern hemisphere, or your seasonal experience is simply different, choose the months that most closely mirror your environment. But enjoy reading them all. You might be called by a prompt that applies to any month, such as observing the night sky.

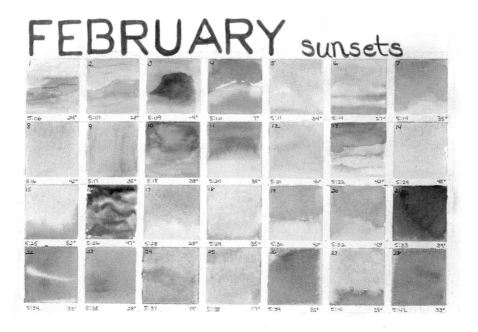

September Daily Prompts

1. Today is the feast day of St. Fiacre, the patron saint of gardeners and herbalists. This Irish saint (607-670) was known for healing with herbs and working miracles. Have you ever experienced the healing power of herbs? Describe your experience in your journal.

2. Express thanks, in any way you wish, for all the healing powers of Mother Earth.

3. Select a deciduous tree to observe through the coming months. Record your first observation.

4. I notice...
   I wonder...
   It reminds me of...

5. As you think of autumn, what words come to mind? List them in your journal.

6. Eco-anxiety is a growing health problem around the world. Do you, or someone you know, experience it? How can the practice of nature journaling help reduce this suffering? Reflect on the possibilities in your journal.

7. Trees and shrubs are showy with leaves, berries, nuts and seeds. Identify and record them.

8. What animals do you see storing food for winter?

9. Follow a flower's journey from bud to bloom, to fade, to death. Record the dates of these changes in color and form.

10. Revisit your tree and sit where you sat on your last visit. This is known as your *sit spot*. In your journal, note any changes in words, numbers, and/or images.

11. Today is the anniversary of 9-11-2001. Read the story of the Callery pear tree, known as the *Survivor Tree*. On this day of remembrance, compose a healing prayer in your journal.

12. Find three varieties of grasses to draw and label them in your journal.

13. Watch your bird feeders for changes in visitors. Check out Project Feeder Watch at the Cornell Lab of Ornithology. See if you can participate as a citizen scientist.

14. As leaves begin to fall, enter a leaf rubbing in your journal.

15. Record weather data and more on a phenology wheel. You can do this in your journal or you can make a separate, stand-alone phenology wheel over the course of a month or a year.
16. Are there any unusual rock formations in your area? Visit and record.
17. Revisit your tree and note any changes.
18. Have you watched a bird cam online? It is an easy, comfortable way to observe live birds up close. www.allaboutbirds. org/cams
19. Watch for dropping leaves. What trees drop theirs first?
20. Look for fungi and identify them. What trees are they under? What are their relationships?
21. Today is World Gratitude Day. Make a list of nature's gifts in your immediate environment that you are grateful for. Pick one to highlight with an image and background information.
22. The Autumn Equinox is arriving at this time of year. Are you aware of the changes of light that are happening? How do the sunrise and sunset today compare with a month ago?
23. What Native Peoples' land(s) do you live on? Map your findings in your journal. If you need assistance, try the Native Land App.
24. Revisit your tree. Note changes. Continue this observation throughout the fall and other seasons too, if you wish.
25. Choose several leaves from different tree species to study. Leaves come in many shapes. Notice the difference in their margins or edges. Note the venation in each leaf. Record your findings.
26. Make a page of the various colors you see in leaves this fall. This could be a simple chart of color squares.
27. Speciesism occurs when we elevate humans over other animals in ways that lead to their mistreatment. This common prejudice can easily creep into our thinking and language. Be aware of this proclivity and check your own journal entries for slipups.
28. Would you like to make your own nature journal? You can get a book of instructions on constructing journals from your local library or check out www.handmadebooksandjournals.com
29. Today is the day we honor Confucius. Here are some inspiring words from him: "Everything has beauty, but not everyone

sees it." How does nature journaling help you see the beauty around you?

30. Create a prayer of praise for autumn.

October Daily Prompts

1. What changes in your environment would you like to track this month? Length of day? Phases of the Moon? Temperatures? Other?
2. You can contribute to our understanding of the planet we call home through citizen science. Search the database on www.citizenscience.gov Your activities as a citizen scientist can make great entries in your journal.
3. Pick a deciduous tree to visit daily this month. Record your observations.
4. Today is the feast day of St. Francis of Assisi, patron saint of animals and the environment. Why do you think this saint is so beloved?
5. Eyes on the skies. How many types of clouds can you identify? Record what you observe.
6. Visit a garden center and look at the wide variety of pumpkins, gourds, and other fall beauties. Pick one to take home and draw.
7. Find a pumpkin recipe for baking. Assemble all the ingredients and then enjoy mindful baking, followed by mindful eating. Share. Give thanks.
8. Take a walk in a nearby park. Find a place to sit quietly. Observe your environment with your senses, concentrating on one at a time. With care look, hear, smell, touch, and taste. Note what you observe through each sensation.
9. Observe the colors of fall leaves. How many do you discover? Do you have a favorite fallen leaf? Press it in your journal.
10. Listen and watch for migrating birds. What do you hear and see?
11. Find a poem about autumn that resonates with you and copy it in your journal.
12. Visit a natural habitat and create a map of it. Label notable places.
13. Watch for the first frost and record it.
14. Some seeds fly. Find examples for your journal.
15. What native flowers are still blooming?
16. Do you see any signs of animals preparing for colder weather?

Do you see any chubby animals? Watch for squirrels gathering nuts for winter. They are often forgetful about where they store their finds, giving an unintentional gift to the environment.

17. All genres of literature celebrate nature. Herman Melville's whale in *Moby Dick*, Mary Oliver's *White Flowers*, Robert Frost's *Birches* and Shel Silverstein's *The Giving Tree* are all famous. Do you have any favorite written works that celebrate the plant or animal kingdoms? Note them in your journal.

18. Do your houseplants need any preparation for the coming months? Perhaps they need to be separated or trimmed, placed in bigger pots, or fed some special food. Remember they are a part of nature too.

19. During autumn the cycle of life ends for many. How do you view this? What emotions arise? Reflect in your journal.

20. Visit a farmers' market and enjoy fall's bounty. Is there a fall treat you can prepare for someone who is ill or lonely?

21. There are many kinds of pinecones. Find one you like, look at it under a magnifying glass, and draw the details.

22. Does the Greek myth of Persephone and Demeter have meaning for you? If so, how?

23. Today the swallows leave San Juan Capistrano Mission in California and head for their winter homes. Do you know the legend of these swallows? Are there birds you no longer see in your neighborhood? Make a list.

24. Today is United Nations Day. How does the UN champion the environment? What can you learn from their work? Write about what resonates most with you.

25. Plant bulbs in your garden now for spring blooms. Or plant some bulbs in pots for winter blooms inside.

26. The United Nations reports that 1,000,000 plant and animal species are now in danger of extinction. Investigate efforts to turn this trend around. Tell the story of the comeback of the bald eagle in the USA, or other encouraging efforts. What can be done?

27. Autumn is a time of letting go. Just as the trees release their leaves, what do you want to release – an emotion, a habit, a relationship? Draw leaves in your journal and on each one say goodbye to something or someone.

28. Sunflowers, native to the Americas, track the sun (heliotropism). See if you can follow a sunflower's path for a day and diagram it in your journal.
29. Create an autumn mandala with leaves you collect. In your journal, create another with words, and/or images.
30. Bats have a bad reputation, but they are beneficial to agriculture and ecosystems. List the ways they are useful beyond Halloween decorations.
31. Halloween springs from the Celtic festival of Samhain. This marks the end of the lighter half of the year. How can you show this time shift in your journal?

November Daily Prompts

1. Today is All Saints Day. If planet Earth could crown some saints, who would she choose? Honor them in your journal.
2. This is the month of Thanksgiving. Why not record one thing you are grateful for each day?
3. Are you feeding the birds this winter? Time to get organized for our feathered friends. Bird feeder visitors can provide a lot of material for your journal.
4. If you live in a cold climate, birds will need clean, fresh water as ice forms. Can you help?
5. Look for the first snow. Be sure to note it in your journal.
6. Take an urban walk. Can you discover nature there? Map your walk and note your findings.
7. Do you have pumpkins left from Halloween? Take them into the woods, break them open, and leave a feast for the wildlife. (Be sure they are not treated in any way.)
8. Raining? Go ahead and take a walk in the rain. What can you record in your journal when you return home?
9. What animals near you are preparing for hibernation. Can you see evidence of this to enter in your journal?
10. This is Native American Heritage Month. Read, or reread *Braiding Sweetgrass*. Choose a quote for your journal.
11. What are Tamaracks or Larches? What makes them unique? Can you visit one in your area?
12. The chrysanthemum is the flower of November. It is important in Eastern cultures, representing joy, longevity, love, loyalty and the sun. It is the national flower of Japan. What is your national flower? Enter it in your journal.
13. Explore the details of a colorful leaf with a magnifying hand lens. Draw the wonders you see.
14. Make a spore print of a mushroom for your journal.
15. Oxfam has declared today International Fast for a World Harvest. Fasting is an ancient tradition in many religions. Have you ever fasted? What was your experience? How does fasting connect us to the Earth? Reflect in your journal.

16. November is World Vegan Month. Explore a plant-based diet to support the planet. Make a plant-based dish to share with a friend.
17. If you are cleaning a yard in preparation for winter, remember to leave some leaves, mulch, and natural areas for wildlife, big and small.
18. Migration is a mystery to us. Study monarch butterflies and let your sense of awe emerge as you learn about this special kind of knowing. Write a blessing for all migrating species on their journeys and place it in your journal.
19. As you prepare for Thanksgiving, remember those sentient beings who are hungry. How can this suffering be alleviated? How can you help?
20. Did you know turkeys have better vision than we do? They are also intelligent, sensitive, and friendly. Forty-six million are killed each year for our Thanksgiving dinner tables. Explore other options. Reflect on turkeys in your journal.
21. Why is Thanksgiving also a National Day of Mourning? What is the history of the land you are standing on? Who are your land ancestors? Check it out on the Native Lands App.
22. Read the Haudenosaunee Thanksgiving Address. Are there exerpts to include in your journal?
23. Are there people who taught you about nature and nature journaling, who increased your awareness and appreciation? Write them a note of thanks. Honor them in your journal.
24. Do you still see flowers blooming? Record them.
25. I notice...
    I wonder...
    It reminds me of...
26. This is the season of buy, buy, buy. What are the environmental consequences of runaway consumerism? Add your reflections to your journal.
27. Take a walk and silently bless every living thing you see.
28. Can you hear migrating birds? Note the frequency and volume of their calls. Diagram them in your journal.
29. The colors of the Earth and sky are changing. Record this transition in your journal using only color.
30. Write a prayer of praise for all sentient beings.

Why is Thanksgiving also a National Day of Mourning? What is the history of the land you are standing on? Who are your land ancestors?

December Daily Prompts

1. This time of year can be hectic. Make a commitment to gift yourself with some time in nature and put it on your calendar. Record your aspiration in your journal.
2. December is a month of darkness. Explore nature in the dark, outdoors, or from the comfort of your seat at a window. Start documenting what you see.
3. This is a great time for observing the night sky. Watch for clear nights that allow you to see constellations. Use apps such as Star Walk or SkyView if you need help with identification.
4. How does the darkness feel to you? Scary? Cozy? Inviting? Mysterious? Write your reflections in your journal.
5. Winter skies are often muted and beautiful. Record any colors, clouds, sunrises and sunsets that interest you.
6. What plants and animals are endangered where you live? How can you help?
7. Are any animals in need in your yard or neighborhood? Document both the need and any assistance you give.
8. Today is the traditional feast day of St. Nicholas. He is famous for his generosity, so this is a good time to reflect on that virtue. How is the Earth generous to you? How are you generous to her?
9. Many Buddhists celebrate Bodhi Day today. It honors the time that Buddha meditated under the Bodhi Tree and attained enlightenment. Do you have a tree that invites you to sit and reflect? Draw it in your journal.
10. "Every single creature is full of God and is a book about God." Meister Eckhart
    Find a creature to observe today and note what you see. Do you experience a spiritual connection?
11. How have you enjoyed your nature journaling this year? Is there something you would like to continue next year? Is there something new you would like to learn about or try? Do you need any supplies to get started? If so, make a plan.
12. Write a haiku to snow for your journal.
13. Today is National Day of the Horse. Research humanity's relationship with this noble being. Document what you find out.

14. Give thanks for the shelter of your home. How are other beings keeping safe in the cold? As you learn, list some ways in your journal.

15. Visit a pond and see if there is any open water. What is alive and what is dead? What is merely sleeping? Draw and label what you see.

16. Are you seeing different birds this winter? Who is visiting? Make a list.

17. Draw the silhouettes of winter's deciduous trees in your journal.

18. This is a quiet time of year. Take a few minutes to sit and listen to the sounds you hear in the winter landscape. Note them in any way you wish.

19. What green plants can you still find? How do they remain green in the deep cold of winter? Investigate and put your findings in your journal.

20. If this is a gift giving time of year for you, consider giving a gift about, or from, nature. Consider a beautiful plant, the planting of a tree, or a book on nature or nature journaling.

21. This is the Winter Solstice. On this longest night of the year, light a candle and give thanks for the returning light of the sun. Record the sun and the moon just as they are today in your journal.

22. In the Celtic tradition, this is a "thin" time. What does that mean to you? Write a reflection or a poem.

23. Visit www.johnmuirlaws.com and read a blog post or watch a video. Be inspired!

24. Is there music that resonates with you and the darkness of this time of year? Make a note of it in your journal.

25. Christmas is the celebration the birth of the Christ Child. He arrived in a shelter that housed animals. Does this detail of his story offer a lesson for today's world? Reflect in your journal.

26. If you could make a wish for the environment, what would it be? How can wishes come true?

27. Take a walk in a city park and see what you discover. If it is too cold to journal outdoors, record what was most interesting when you return home.

28. Too cold to go outside? Visit your refrigerator and pull out a gift from the earth. How did it reach you? How far did it travel? How many people were involved from its origin to your frig. Note your findings in words, images, and/or numbers. Consider including a map.
29. What is the most valuable thing you have discovered through nature journaling this year?
30. Share your nature journal with a friend. Invite your friend to join you in this practice.
31. Take out your journal and look at all you have recorded this year. Give thanks!

January Daily Prompts

1. Name three aspirations for the new year. List them in your journal.
2. Are you beginning a new journal with the new calendar year? Why not consider keeping a perpetual nature journal for 3, 5, or even 10 years? It can be weekly, biweekly, or monthly. It is a great way to review your experiences over time.
3. We are at Earth's perihelion. Record what that means in your journal. Draw a diagram. Write a poem to honor the sun.
4. It is possible to journal online. If that appeals to you, give it a try.
5. Today is National Bird Day. Observe a bird. What is this being teaching you? Record the lessons in your journal.
6. Give thanks for the winged ones and birdsong. Make a pine-cone bird feeder for them.
7. Imagine all the life beneath the snow. What do you see? Make a diagram of life underground.
8. When can you see the Wolf Moon? How did it get its name? Why do wolves howl? Record your findings.
9. Winter is a good time to visit museums. Find an art museum and look at the works that celebrate nature. If allowed, do your own drawing there, or complete your journal entry at home.
10. How many kinds of evergreens can you identify? Draw and label them.
11. Do you want to be inspired? Watch a David Attenborough documentary.
12. Can you find any evidence of animal or bird tracks? Draw and label them in your journal.
13. Observe a body of water, open or frozen. What do you see? Document your findings.
14. Find several twigs and examine them with a magnifying glass. Compare and contrast them in your journal.
15. Today is Martin Luther King's birthday. How can we extend his quest for freedom to all sentient beings?
16. "All of life is interrelated." (MLK Jr.) In your journal, list some ways you witness this truth.

17. Visit W. A. Bentley online. Draw a snowflake. Explore the sacred geometry.
18. Along the West Coast of North American, gray whales are migrating. Give thanks for clear water and all sea life.
19. Visit a city park and record what draws your attention.
20. Look for patterns in the frost on windows. What is frost? Draw the patterns you see.
21. Play! Make a snow person or snow angel.
22. I notice...
    I wonder...
    It reminds me of...
23. Step outside and do walking meditation. Bless the Earth with each step.
24. Give thanks for all trees and plants.
25. Albert Einstein said, "There are only two ways to live your life. One is as though nothing is a miracle. The other is as though everything is a miracle." Witness a miracle today. Record it in your journal with words, pictures and/or numbers.
26. Watch the sky today. Note the qualities of winter's light.
27. Study the sky with a telescope. What do you see?
28. This is the season of Tu B'Shevat, the Jewish new year for trees. Visit a tree you love and honor it in your journal.
29. Sit by a window in the dark of night and look at the trees. Draw or write a poem to honor them.
30. Is there snow outside? How many colors do you see in it? Enter them in your journal.
31. Create a prayer in praise of snow or the season of winter.

February Daily Prompts

1. Watch for Brigid's snowdrops to appear. Today is her feast day and marks the arrival of spring in Ireland. Do you see signs of spring in your neighborhood?
2. This Groundhog Day learn about the real life of a woodchuck and record your findings.
3. Write a meditation on winter.
4. Can you find a dried, dead leaf? Look at it deeply. Reflect on it in your journal.
5. This month some birds begin to mate. Document the signs of courtship you observe.
6. Give thanks for the moon and stars. When can you see the Snow Moon, also known as the Hunger Moon? Where do those names come from?
7. Name and draw a star constellation in your journal. Why did you select this particular constellation?
8. Sit before the fire in your fireplace, or gaze at a simple candle's flame. What are the gifts? Give thanks for fire in your journal.
9. Jane Goodall said, "What you do makes a difference, and you have to decide what kind of difference you want to make." Listen to a Jane Goodall TED Talk. Get inspired!
10. Look for open water and watch the ducks. Feed them peas thawed from frozen. Record your experience in words, images, and/or numbers.
11. This is the time of year of the Chinese Lantern Festival, the festival of lights. Write a lantern poem for your journal.
12. Are you strongly connected to a four-legged one? Write a tribute in your journal and add a drawing or picture.
13. Visit a garden center. Note your observations.
14. Sit by a window and have a mindful cup of tea as you observe the outdoors.
15. In your journal, give thanks for all the opportunities you have to love Mother Earth this Valentine's Day.
16. Write a letter of support to legislators and influencers championing environmental reforms and protections.
17. Create an altar made of gifts from nature. Enter it in your

journal in words and/or pictures.

18. Watch the sunset. Record time, weather, and colors.
19. Examine the colors and lines of any plant with a magnifying glass. What do you find?
20. Does this winter season seem different from the winters of your childhood? If so, how? List the changes in your journal and reflect on them.
21. Bless a small creature. Write the blessing in your journal.
22. Go outside. Close your eyes. Listen. Record what you hear.
23. You are made of stardust. What does this statement mean to you? Reflect in your journal.
24. The arts are an important means of communication. What is environmental art? Research an environmental artist and honor that artist in your journal.
25. Look for mosses. How many kinds can you discover? Use a magnifying glass to see them clearly and note your findings.
26. Who is emerging from a long winter's nap?
27. What is greenwashing? How is it impacting the environment? Give an example in your journal.
28. Create a prayer in praise of all animals.
29. Give thanks for our Indigenous ancestors.

March Daily Prompts

1. Today is the anniversary of Yellowstone National Park. Do you have a favorite park? Pay tribute to it in your journal.
2. Can you find green in the bark of trees? Note these sightings.
3. Nature evolves quickly with the arrival of spring. Pick a single subject and document the changes in the weeks ahead.
4. Visit the Wild Wonder Foundation online. www.wildwonder. org Be sure to check out all the announcements and the calendar of events.
5. Take a journey and look at nature in a setting new to you. Record your discoveries in words, pictures, and/or numbers.
6. Make a list of the signs of spring you see. What does spring stir in you? Write a poem for your journal.
7. Give thanks for environmental activists.
8. Visit a "thin" place this week. What does this experience awaken in you?
9. It is mud season. Inspect some mud remembering the Buddhist teaching – No Mud, No Lotus! What do these words of wisdom mean in your life?
10. Record all the birds you see. Eggs are in nests this month. What do you wish to birth? Record your reflections in your journal.
11. Today is Johnny Appleseed Day. Investigate the agricultural practices of orchards where you live.
12. Revisit Rachel Carson and her seminal writings. Find a quote from her for your journal.
13. Witness the return of Canadian geese. Listen to their call.
14. How is the air quality where you live? Record your findings. Give thanks for fresh air.
15. Find an insect and study it with a magnifying glass. Honor all creepy crawlies in your journal.
16. Is there a planetarium near you? Plan a visit and create a journal entry based on what you learn there.
17. Discover the history of the shamrock tradition. What plant symbol is meaningful to you?
18. Build a cairn in the woods or a city park. Be careful not to disturb small beings.

19. At this time of year, the swallows return to San Juan Capistrano for the summer. Who is returning to your neighborhood?

20. Rise and greet the dawn. Note what you observe as this day begins.

21. Give thanks for changing seasons. This is the time of the Vernal Equinox, marking an equal balance between light and darkness. Record the times of sunrise and sunset.

22. Shinrin-yoku translates from Japanese to "forest bathing" in English. This is the practice of going outside to promote healing; it is part of Japan's health program. Have you experienced healing in nature? Reflect in your journal.

23. Plan your flower garden. Consider pollinators, biodiversity, and all the many possibilities that come with gardening. Get some seeds started indoors and begin a record of your plants in your journal.

24. What are the threats to bees and butterflies? What can you do to protect them?

25. Visit a sugarhouse. What gifts of food do you most enjoy from Mother Earth? Make a list in your journal.

26. Shop at the farmers' market near you. Eat only plants today, locally grown if possible. Put a favorite plant-based recipe in your journal.

27. "The greatest of human discoveries in the future will be the discovery of human intimacy with all those other modes of being that live with us on this planet, inspire our art and literature, reveal that numinous world whence all things came into being, and with which we exchange the very substance of life." Thomas Berry (1914-2009) Do you agree with Thomas Berry? If so, how does nature journaling contribute to this great discovery?

28. Listen for the peepers' song and note it. Does it bring back any memories from your childhood? Do other sounds?

29. Create a nature journaling kit for a child. You will need a journal with blank pages, a pencil, eraser, and perhaps some colored pencils or markers. A magnifying glass is a great addition. Then give this gift to a child and open up their world to nature journaling.

30. What gift can you give back to Mother Earth today?

31. Create a prayer in praise of pollinators.

April Daily Prompts

1. How many shades of green can you identify this month? Make a chart of greens in your journal.
2. Research Hildegard of Bingen's *viriditas*, the greening power of the Divine. Give thanks for Hildegard and all our teachers. Honor a teacher in your journal.
3. Is it true that it rains a lot in April? Record the daily rainfall this month.
4. Rainbows come with the rain. Many cultures have charming stories and beliefs about these beautiful occurrences. What does a rainbow mean to you? Keep your eye out for one to place in your journal.
5. As the world becomes more colorful, draw a color wheel of primary and secondary colors. List all the places you find each color in nature. If you like this challenge, add the tertiary colors.
6. Look for emerging friends, such as moles and chipmunks. Record your sightings.
7. Look for buds on bushes, shrubs and trees. Watch for spring sprouts and note where you first see them. Track their growth and note their many varieties. Later you can identify them. The app iNaturalist is a great help.
8. Look for the buds of flowers. Buds are full of promise, just like you. Reflect in your journal on areas of growth within yourself you want to nurture.
9. This is mating season for many birds and other animals. Do you see any signs to include in your journal?
10. Take a walk in an area you have not visited during the winter months. Discover it anew.
11. Look for feathers on your walks. Can you identify them? If you need some help, there is a Feather Atlas on the website of the US Fish and Wildlife Service. www.fws.gov Record your findings in words, images, and/or numbers.
12. Are you going to plant a vegetable garden? Whether it is on an acre or in a small container, this is the time to plan. Use your journal to help you get organized.
13. Today is National Dolphin Day, a time to celebrate all sea

creatures. Visit the ocean or an aquarium. Design a journal page based on your discoveries.

14. Can you create a page in the style of a comic strip?

15. The days are getting longer. Do you notice any change in your energy?

16. Begin your morning listening to birdsong. Are you hearing new melodies or some old favorites? Use the Merlin App if you need help identifying the birds. List the ones you hear in your journal. You can also make a note of the birds you see, as well as hear.

17. Keep watch from your sit spot near one deciduous tree as it greens and buds. Record what you see.

18. Tonight, look up at the sky and spend some time in reflection.

19. Take a plant (or shell, flowers, or any gift from nature) to someone who is shut in.

20. Today is the birthday of John Muir, advocate of forests. Gift the planting of a tree to someone special and record it in your journal.

21. Do you know who US Senator Gaylord Nelson is? Note his contributions to the environment in your journal.

22. Earth Day! Celebrate! Bring her a special gift on her day. Why not join an environmental service project in your community?

23. Do you see any nests being built? Have you seen a fly, bee, or bug?

24. Keep watch and make your journal entries at a respectful distance.

25. Is there a body of water near you? What changes do you observe there? Document what you see.

26. Today is the birthday of John James Audubon, ornithologist and artist. In tribute to him, study and draw a bird you observe today.

27. Visit an old stone wall. How many lifeforms are present? What else do you find for your journal?

28. How do you cultivate your curiosity? List three things you would like to lean more about. For each one, make a list of questions to explore. Have fun with your lists.

29. Research what plants and animals near you are endangered. What actions can you take to help protect them?

30. Give thanks for longer days to go exploring.

May Daily Prompts

1. Worms are hungry creatures who can eat their own weight every day. They build important tunnels in the ground. Discover how they contribute to soil health, and therefore to us. Diagram this ecosystem in your journal.
2. May is the month of flowers. List ten common ones around you now.
3. Who is the Goddess Maia and why does the month of May carry her name?
4. Draw a simple flower with many petals. On each petal, write the name of someone you are grateful for. Repeat this exercise, but this time offer gratitude for other gifts of nature.
5. The first week of May is Be Kind to Animals Week. Can you find a way to offer kindness to wild animals and/or a pet?
6. Create a graphic plan for the garden of your dreams.
7. Springtime is a burst of color. Fill a page of your journal with squares of various colors and their many shades.
8. Visit a pond or another body of water. Record what you see. Can you locate any new life to regularly visit over the weeks ahead?
9. Make a reference chart of common birds' eggs. Keep your eyes open for them.
10. Select three birds' nests to study. Note their variety. Record their sizes, locations, materials, and any other interesting features.
11. Horticultural therapy has existed since ancient times. Now it is a recognized profession. What can you learn about this growing field? How does it relate to nature journaling?
12. Create a May basket and hang it on a friend's door. Consider making it an anonymous gift.
13. Where are you spotting springtime's flowers? Make a map in your journal identifying their locations.
14. Julian of Norwich tells us, "The fullness of joy is to behold God in everything." Where do you find joy today?
15. I notice...
    I wonder...
    It reminds me of...

16. Today is the feast day of St. Brendan the Navigator. He is the patron saint of whales. Do you know why? Is his story still important today?

17. When you are out in nature, don't forget to take a close-up view and a wide-angle view. This zooming in and out will bring you a varied and rich experience.

18. Pick a plant, or more than one, to follow through its life cycle. Enter your observations in your journal.

19. Find a farmer whose practices support biodiversity. Become a customer and spread the word.

20. Explore the geometry of flowers. Can you see circles, triangles, rectangles, or other shapes? Draw your findings in your journal.

21. Black Elk taught, "The power of the World always works in circles, and everything tries to be round... The sky is round and I have heard the earth is round like a ball, and so are all the stars. The wind in its greatest powers whirls, birds make their nests in circles, for theirs is the same religion as ours." Draw a mandala in honor of Black Elk today.

22. Explore the simple dandelion. How does it represent the sun, moon, and stars through its life cycle? Draw these three stages of its life in your journal.

23. How can the humble dandelion be used for food (for humans and others), medicine, dye, and decoration? Note your findings.

24. Millions of dollars are spent every year on pesticides to kill dandelions. How can this practice be changed?

25. Are there ticks near you? Do they carry diseases? Do you know how to protect yourself and others?

26. Find a tree that speaks to you and look at it slowly from all sides. As you move, how does it appear the same and how is it different? What does this tell you about perspective? Record your findings.

27. Explore the flowers of the artist Georgia O'Keeffe. What did you learn?

28. Dissect a flower. Can you identify leaves, petals, stem, stigma, pistil, stamen, anther, receptacle, filament, ovary or other parts? Draw and label your dissection.

29. Many cultures associate flowers with sentient beings'

attributes. What flowers come to mind when you think of love, courage, faithfulness, joy, grief, or hope? Create a list with images in your journal.

30. Is there a pattern in nature you would like to track in June? Make a plan today.
31. Create a prayer in praise of flowers.

June Daily Prompts

1. Do you have a spirit animal? Describe that experience in your journal.
2. If you have the opportunity, explore the amazing underwater world of large lakes, rivers or the oceans. Reflect on the wonders you witness.
3. Take a walk in nature. Find a place to sit; close your eyes and note what you hear. Record the sounds in your journal.
4. Today is Rosalia Day, the ancient festival of roses in Rome. Explore the various wild and cultivated varieties. What did you learn?
5. Butterflies have arrived. Keep a record of the ones you see.
6. What butterflies are endangered in your region? What can be done to support them?
7. Research the various types of birds' nests. Locate one and watch for fledglings.
8. Have you seen any beetles? Study them and put your findings in your journal.
9. Ferns are among our oldest plants, some species dating back 360 million years. Press and draw any ferns you find. Note their spores.
10. Have you planted a garden or simply visited one? Is there a community garden near you? Small or large, all gardens yield many benefits. List the ones you can think of in your journal.
11. Dedicate a page to just one color. What can you find in nature in various shades of that single color?
12. Before photography, scientists depended on their artistic abilities to record their findings. This became a doorway for women into science, a field that was almost always closed to them. An early, extraordinary naturalist and scientist is Maria Sibylla Merian (1647-1717). Read about her interesting life and be inspired. What contemporary figures influence your nature journaling?
13. In order to see and hear, we must quiet our days. Experiment with divorcing from technology even for one day. What is your experience?

14. Go to the farmers' market and try something new to eat. Write a blessing for all farmers.
15. Enjoy eating a meal outdoors today. Record what you notice.
16. Are there wildflowers in your neighborhood? Many wildflowers have medicinal properties. Document your findings.
17. Watch for a murmuration of birds. Using just dots to represent them, draw the design(s) of their show in your journal.
18. Birds are building their nests. Can you place any materials out to help? Examples: dried twigs, pine needles, mosses.
19. Rainy day? Watch a nature documentary and get inspired.
20. From the Tao: "The world is a sacred vessel that cannot be changed. He who changes it will destroy it. He who seizes it will lose it." What does this quote mean to you? Reflect in your journal.
21. It is the Summer Solstice, the longest day of the year. It is a time of festivals to celebrate the power of the sun. Record sunrise and sunset times. What colors do you see?
22. Today is World Rainforest Day. What are some of your favorite rainforest life forms? Express your awe in your journal in images, words, and/or numbers.
23. Go outdoors on a warm night and pick a constellation to draw in your journal. What else do you see? Are there any fireflies? How do they light up?
24. Today is Inti Raymi, the ancient Inca Festival of the Sun. Express your gratitude and praise for this life source. Give thanks for light in all its forms.
25. Watch for thunderstorms. After one passes by, go outside and notice the air. Describe it in your journal.
26. Would your houseplants like some time outside? Notice how they do in different settings.
27. Find some goldenrod or milkweed plants and record the insects you see there in words, images, and/or numbers.
28. Is your vegetable garden blooming? Share the produce with a friend. Have a bumper crop? Share it with the local food pantry.
29. Lush summer months can give us a false sense of environmental stability. Note your concerns for the Earth in your journal and look for a stewardship project to join.
30. Write a prayer of praise for nature's bounty.

July Daily Prompts

1. Are you taking a summer vacation? Map your journey in your journal. Make a map key and note landscape features.
2. Before you leave home, research what the natural world offers in the places you visit, even urban locations. What does your trip offer in landscapes, flora and fauna? Don't forget to pack your journaling supplies.
3. Visit the website of the Land Institute. https://landinstitude.org How does their important work impact nature and your future? Record what you learn in your journal.
4. Do you know what plant blindness is? How can you help those who suffer with this condition?
5. Make a weekly visit to your sit spot this month. What relationships do you see among all the many forms of life? Diagram them in your journal.
6. Stop and look at the verges of a busy highway. Despite all the traffic, what do you find growing there? Record these resilient beings in words, images, and numbers.
7. Find a plant with strong lines of form. Then draw the plant in your journal while looking only at the plant, not the journal. What did you learn?
8. Visit a pond and look for new duck families. Return at the end of the month and note the ducklings' growth.
9. Visit a farmstand and pick a vegetable or fruit to celebrate in your journal. Draw it from various angles and draw a cross-section. Label all parts.
10. Can you get out on the water in a boat, or take a swim? What do you see to journal about?
11. Today is World Population Day. Do you know how many humans are on the planet? Record your answer and your reflections.
12. Find a beautiful plant or animal and practice *visio divina*. Record your experience.
13. Find a photograph of your city park from a century ago. How has it changed? Record what seems positive and negative about those changes.

14. Squirrels are busy playing with one another. Note their many antics in your journal.
15. Visit a family farm and pick your own berries. Pick some for a neighbor too.
16. Write an acrostic poem for your journal celebrating the beauty of summer.
17. During this time of bounty, observe and list all of nature's gifts to you. Choose one or two to draw. Express your gratitude.
18. Beethoven's sixth symphony, the "Pastoral," is his musical description of a summer day in the countryside. Listen to it and journal about your impressions. What other music do you associate with this season? From Beethoven to the Beach Boys, there are choices to brighten everyone's days.
19. Open your Merlin App and note all the many birds singing to you in your own back yard. Which birds can you see, and which ones remain hidden? Make a chart.
20. Create a way to note birdsong. It only has to make sense to you.
21. Are you visiting a beach this summer? Take along a bag to pick up any refuse. You are a steward of this Earth. Record beach conditions in your journal.
22. There are many kinds of seaweed. Can you identify any and enter them in your journal?
23. The Western Abenaki named July's full moon, the Thunder Moon. This name acknowledges the likelihood of thunderstorms at this time of year. What is your experience of lightning and thunder? A warning? A threat? Other reactions?
24. Indigenous peoples have long planted crops in a grouping called the Three Sisters. Research this practice. Why is it so popular and what does it teach us? If you have a garden, why not plant a Three Sisters bed? Or simply draw and describe one in your journal.
25. Find a recipe for the Three Sisters and prepare it. Record your experience.
26. There is an ancient Celtic tradition of "telling the bees." Bees were seen as a link between worlds. All of life's major events, such as births, marriages and deaths, were whispered to them by their keepers. After loved ones' deaths, messages were passed to the deceased by telling the bees. Who do you

talk to in the natural world? Who gives you solace? Honor them in your journal.

27. There are many species of bees. How many live in your locality? Make a list with identifying details.

28. What is the difference between solitary and hive bees? Keep note of your observations and research.

29. Shells are so diverse and beautiful. If you are fortunate to visit a beach, record the shells you find.

30. If you spot a sand crab sticking its head out of the sand, sit down and watch it for a while. You will be entertained and have fun recording this little creature. Did you know crabs have been on the Earth for over 450 million years?

31. What are the natural sources of light and what are their gifts to you? Write a prayer in praise of light.

August Daily Prompts

1. The beginning of August brings the Celtic festival of Lughnasa. It is the first of this culture's annual harvest festivals. What is being harvested in your area? What are you harvesting in your own life? Reflect in your journal.

2. Midsummer can bring dangerously hot weather for all living beings. How can you contribute to their relief? Create a shelter? Offer water?

3. Hummingbirds are amazing creatures. These tiny beings migrate thousands of miles and fly backward, forward and hover. They inspired the design of helicopters. Put up a feeder for them, or plant their favorite flowers, and enjoy their friendly visits.

4. Roadsides and fields are full of wildflowers. Select some to record in your journal.

5. Press some wildflowers to draw in the winter months. List their locations and the dates found.

6. Visit a pond and see if you spot any turtles or frogs. Some snakes like to sunbathe. Check out rocks for these sun worshippers. Enter your findings in your journal.

7. Today is the anniversary of the first photo of Earth from space. Reflect in your journal on seeing the planet from that perspective.

8. Do you know how ladybugs are helpful? See if you can spot one. Note your findings.

9. Today is the International Day of World's Indigenous People. Here is some inspiration for your journaling.
   "Our spirituality is a oneness and an interconnectedness with all that lives and breathes...Even with all that does not live or breathe." Mudrooroo Narogin (Australia)

10. Visit a park, sit down and close your eyes. Record anything you smell and every sound you hear.

11. Are there animals you are ambivalent about or find abhorrent? See what you can learn about them, through direct observation and/or research. What has caused your feelings? Reflect on your findings in your journal.

12. Insects are everywhere. Can you see their beauty and

appreciate their contributions? Record your findings.

13. Lean back and watch the clouds in the sky. Do their forms remind you of anything? Label the different formations and research what they tell us about the weather and atmosphere.

14. Visit a state or federal park. What did you see? What did you learn?

15. Today is International Homeless Animals Day. Visit an animal shelter. Take a gift.

16. Find a quiet place to sit and observe the natural world. Record all the relationships you can see. Diagram them.

17. Write a poem about the connecting web you observed yesterday.

18. Recall your earliest memory in the natural world. Reflect on that time and create an entry for your journal.

19. Take some children on a walk. Listen to the young. Try to see your surroundings through their eyes. Invite them to journal with you.

20. Watch the movement of a small animal or bird. In your journal, draw quick sketches of your subject in as many positions as you can. What are you seeing?

21. Make a picnic of plant-based foods. Invite a loved one and share a beautiful day in nature.

22. Today is World Plant Milk Day. What plant milks have you tried? What is the impact of each on the environment? What is the impact of dairy farming? Create a chart about the various milks, including your favorite.

23. Nature is full of patterns. Find an interesting pattern and record it.

24. Questioning is an important part of observing nature. Are you puzzled by what you see? Record all your questions to research later.

25. What temperatures are being recorded this month in your locality? Note any reactions you have.

26. Do you have a favorite river, lake, or ocean? Create a page to celebrate it.

27. Notice and record the plants, birds, and/or animals attracted to waterways in your area.

28. Do waterways near you have invasive species? What is being done to manage the problem? Are there stewardship

programs where you can help?

29. What is the water quality where you live? Record the details.

30. Many folks are making a last summer trip to the beach this week. Do you have a favorite beach? Place a description and image in your journal. Perhaps there are special memories or a poem you'd like to include.

31. Write a prayer in praise of water.

Acknowledgments

This book is a celebration of the web of life. Writing it was part of that celebration. There are so many to thank, and I do so with a full and happy heart.

First, and foremost, are the teachers. Without them, the world of nature journaling would never have opened to me. Although I have never met Jack Laws in person, he is the linchpin that made it all possible. I had been a longtime keeper of journals, but I had never heard of nature journals. From Jack I learned that it is a rich world of possibilities, and that it is a place where all are invited to flourish. He has a great team infused with enthusiasm and kindness, including Yvea Eaton-Moore who is the definition of radical hospitality.

Ida Mitrani is a Turkish born French artist who lives in Ireland. For two years, she instructed me skillfully in botanical art across the many miles that separated us. Her encouragement has allowed me to persevere in the work of making art, becoming comfortable with my efforts. Now I am fortunate to call her my friend.

A deep bow of thanks to Thich Nhat Hanh and the entire international community of Plum Village. It is there that I learned the life-changing lesson of mindfulness. I continue to reap the benefits of all the practices Thay taught, and to enjoy the spiritual support of my local community, Kingfisher Sangha. A second bow of gratitude goes to my seminary, One Spirit Interfaith Seminary, which continues to nourish my spiritual life through the years.

This book was also made possible by my local nature journaling club. We began during the pandemic by gathering weekly on Zoom to share our love of nature. Now we continue to meet on Zoom monthly, and take day trips to share the joy of journaling together. This group of wonderful journalers has taught me a great deal, and that wisdom is shared in this work. Treasured companions on this path, near and far, have helped me sustain a regular practice, and brought me great joy.

Like most authors, I invite friends to read the drafts as I work. It is a big ask, and I owe a great debt to Shannon Snyder and Sharon Therriault for their sharp eyes and dedicated attention. They made this a better book.

My dear friend, Ali Trowbridge recommended DartFrog Books to me when I was writing *Divine Sparks: Interfaith Wisdom for a Postmodern World*. Her brother, Gordon McClellan, is the founder of DartFrog and its chief executive officer. Gordon's enthusiasm and many skills have created a team that authors can trust. Another great team I have relied on for a long time, is McGreevy ProLab and ProPress in Albany, New York. They did an outstanding job of photographing and digitalizing the artwork for this book. Going from manuscript to book-in-hand is a many-faceted process. I am grateful to both DartFrog and ProLab for their professional expertise.

And behind all I do, at least the best parts, is Tom. He is my first reader, cheerleader, and love. There are no words to express the depths of my gratitude to him.

And to you esteemed reader, I also extend my thanks. Samuel Johnson wrote, "A writer only begins a book. A reader finishes it." Thank you for completing the work. May we strive together to make this glorious planet a peaceful place of sanctuary for all beings.

Made in the USA
Columbia, SC
19 December 2024

7f263585-1b7e-4ce4-a7c7-de82f01cd125R01